-The Great Domain Rush-
Four Points & Factors for Domain Name Disputes in China
By: Dale D. McGinnis

People will do almost anything for property rights or gold. The proof is in the pudding. For instance the

1. "Rushes to Statehood, The Oklahoma Land Runs". Dickinson Research Center. Retrieved 2014-05-09. 2. Reeves, Keir; Frost, Lionel; Fahey, Charles (2010). "Integrating the Historiography of the Nineteenth-Century Gold Rushes". *Australian Economic History Review* 50 (2): 111. 3. (ICANN, 2000). 4. & 5. Article 15 & 16 of CNDRP and rules 6. Article PRC'S Civil Procedure 7. New Rules for Resolving Chinese Domain Name Disputes - A Comparative Analysis Richard WuSchool of LawUniversity of Hong Kong 8. New Rules for Resolving Chinese Domain Name Disputes - A Comparative Analysis Richard WuSchool of LawUniversity of Hong Kong 9. Rule 2(2) CDNDRP and rules 10. CDNDRP and rules 11. "Contracting Parties to the Paris Convention". WIPO. Retrieved 2012-12-30.

12. http://www.wipo.int/treaties/en/text.jsp?file_id=288514 Paris Conventionfor the Protection of Industrial Property of March 20, 1883,as revised at Brussels on December 14, 1900,at Washington on June 2, 1911,at The Hague on November 6, 1925,at London on June 2, 1934,at Lisbon on October 31, 1958,and at Stockholm on July 14, 1967,and as amended on September 28, 1979 13. See id. 14. Alternative Dispute Resolution, An Essential Competency for Lawyers, by Mark V.B. Partridge **Oxford University Press (2009). 15.** http://www.ccpit-patent.com.cn/references/Law_Against_Unfair_Competition_China.htm law Against Unfair Competition of The People's Republic of China (Adopted at the Third Session of the Standing Committee of the Eighth National People's Congress on September 2, 1993. Promulgated by Order No. 10 of the President of the People's Republic of China on September 2, 1993. and Effective as of December 1, General Principles of THE Civil Law of the People's Republic of China (Adopted on April 12, 1986) **16, 17, & 18.** Alternative Dispute Resolution, An Essential Competency for Lawyers, by Mark V.B. Partridge **Oxford University Press (2009).**

Oklahoma Land Rushes of 1889 and 1893, where people migrated from all over United States staking a claim to land. (1) And in the 19th century, were there were Gold Rushes in Australia, New Zealand, Brazil, Canada, South Africa, and the United States, where people in a 'free for all' fever

1. "Rushes to Statehood, The Oklahoma Land Runs". Dickinson Research Center. Retrieved 2014-05-09. 2. Reeves, Keir; Frost, Lionel; Fahey, Charles (2010). "Integrating the Historiography of the Nineteenth-Century Gold Rushes". *Australian Economic History Review* 50 (2): 111. 3. (ICANN, 2000). 4. & 5. Article 15 & 16 of CNDRP and rules
6. Article PRC'S Civil Procedure 7. New Rules for Resolving Chinese Domain Name Disputes - A Comparative Analysis Richard WuSchool of LawUniversity of Hong Kong 8. New Rules for Resolving Chinese Domain Name Disputes - A Comparative Analysis Richard WuSchool of LawUniversity of Hong Kong 9. Rule 2(2) CDNDRP and rules 10. CDNDRP and rules 11. "Contracting Parties to the Paris Convention". WIPO. Retrieved 2012-12-30.

12. http://www.wipo.int/treaties/en/text.jsp?file_id=288514 Paris Conventionfor the Protection of Industrial Property of March 20, 1883,as revised at Brussels on December 14, 1900,at Washington on June 2, 1911,at The Hague on November 6, 1925,at London on June 2, 1934,at Lisbon on October 31, 1958,and at Stockholm on July 14, 1967,and as amended on September 28, 1979 13. See id. 14. Alternative Dispute Resolution, An Essential Competency for Lawyers, by Mark V.B. Partridge **Oxford University Press (2009). 15.** http://www.ccpit-patent.com.cn/references/Law_Against_Unfair_Competition_China.htm law Against Unfair Competition of The People's Republic of China (Adopted at the Third Session of the Standing Committee of the Eighth National People's Congress on September 2, 1993. Promulgated by Order No. 10 of the President of the People's Republic of China on September 2, 1993. and Effective as of December 1, General Principles of THE Civil Law of the People's Republic of China (Adopted on April 12, 1986) **16, 17, & 18.** Alternative Dispute Resolution, An Essential Competency for Lawyers, by Mark V.B. Partridge **Oxford University Press (2009).**

migrated to areas thought to have large gold deposits in order to mine and buy land. (2) In these situations and circumstances, squatting on their right was the 'thing to do'. Various issues sprung up throughout history concerning those rights, and laws were created to protect them.

1. "Rushes to Statehood, The Oklahoma Land Runs". Dickinson Research Center. Retrieved 2014-05-09. 2. Reeves, Keir; Frost, Lionel; Fahey, Charles (2010). "Integrating the Historiography of the Nineteenth-Century Gold Rushes". *Australian Economic History Review* 50 (2): 111. 3. (ICANN, 2000). 4. & 5. Article 15 & 16 of CNDRP and rules
6. Article PRC'S Civil Procedure 7. New Rules for Resolving Chinese Domain Name Disputes - A Comparative Analysis Richard WuSchool of LawUniversity of Hong Kong 8. New Rules for Resolving Chinese Domain Name Disputes - A Comparative Analysis Richard WuSchool of LawUniversity of Hong Kong 9. Rule 2(2) CDNDRP and rules 10. CDNDRP and rules 11. "Contracting Parties to the Paris Convention". WIPO. Retrieved 2012-12-30.

12. http://www.wipo.int/treaties/en/text.jsp?file_id=288514 Paris Conventionfor the Protection of Industrial Property of March 20, 1883,as revised at Brussels on December 14, 1900,at Washington on June 2, 1911,at The Hague on November 6, 1925,at London on June 2, 1934,at Lisbon on October 31, 1958,and at Stockholm on July 14, 1967,and as amended on September 28, 1979 13. See id. 14. Alternative Dispute Resolution, An Essential Competency for Lawyers, by Mark V.B. Partridge **Oxford University Press (2009).** 15. http://www.ccpit-patent.com.cn/references/Law_Against_Unfair_Competition_China.htm law Against Unfair Competition of The People's Republic of China (Adopted at the Third Session of the Standing Committee of the Eighth National People's Congress on September 2, 1993. Promulgated by Order No. 10 of the President of the People's Republic of China on September 2, 1993. and Effective as of December 1, General Principles of THE Civil Law of the People's Republic of China (Adopted on April 12, 1986) **16, 17, & 18.** Alternative Dispute Resolution, An Essential Competency for Lawyers, by Mark V.B. Partridge **Oxford University Press (2009).**

However with the exploration of the inter-web, a new rush for property rights and gold was discovered- The Great Domain Rush. The Internet is tremendously expansive. In fact, one could argue there are an infinite number of possibilities for domain names.

1. "Rushes to Statehood, The Oklahoma Land Runs". Dickinson Research Center. Retrieved 2014-05-09. 2. Reeves, Keir; Frost, Lionel; Fahey, Charles (2010). "Integrating the Historiography of the Nineteenth-Century Gold Rushes". *Australian Economic History Review* 50 (2): 111. 3. (ICANN, 2000). 4. & 5. Article 15 & 16 of CNDRP and rules
6. Article PRC'S Civil Procedure 7. New Rules for Resolving Chinese Domain Name Disputes - A Comparative Analysis Richard WuSchool of LawUniversity of Hong Kong 8. New Rules for Resolving Chinese Domain Name Disputes - A Comparative Analysis Richard WuSchool of LawUniversity of Hong Kong 9. Rule 2(2) CDNDRP and rules 10. CDNDRP and rules 11. "Contracting Parties to the Paris Convention". WIPO. Retrieved 2012-12-30.

12. http://www.wipo.int/treaties/en/text.jsp?file_id=288514 Paris Conventionfor the Protection of Industrial Property of March 20, 1883,as revised at Brussels on December 14, 1900,at Washington on June 2, 1911,at The Hague on November 6, 1925,at London on June 2, 1934,at Lisbon on October 31, 1958,and at Stockholm on July 14, 1967,and as amended on September 28, 1979 13. See id. 14. Alternative Dispute Resolution, An Essential Competency for Lawyers, by Mark V.B. Partridge **Oxford University Press (2009). 15.** http://www.ccpit-patent.com.cn/references/Law_Against_Unfair_Competition_China.htm law Against Unfair Competition of The People's Republic of China (Adopted at the Third Session of the Standing Committee of the Eighth National People's Congress on September 2, 1993. Promulgated by Order No. 10 of the President of the People's Republic of China on September 2, 1993. and Effective as of December 1, General Principles of THE Civil Law of the People's Republic of China (Adopted on April 12, 1986) **16, 17, & 18.** Alternative Dispute Resolution, An Essential Competency for Lawyers, by Mark V.B. Partridge **Oxford University Press (2009).**

However, a commercial enterprise baring a unique name or trademark, will want that specific mark because its consumers and trade industry recognize it by that mark. There in lies the problem. Unlike the typical Gold rusher or Land rusher, staking a claim to a domain name or web page

1. "Rushes to Statehood, The Oklahoma Land Runs". Dickinson Research Center. Retrieved 2014-05-09. 2. Reeves, Keir; Frost, Lionel; Fahey, Charles (2010). "Integrating the Historiography of the Nineteenth-Century Gold Rushes". *Australian Economic History Review* **50** (2): 111. 3. (ICANN, 2000). **4. & 5.** Article 15 & 16 of CNDRP and rules
6. Article PRC'S Civil Procedure 7. New Rules for Resolving Chinese Domain Name Disputes - A Comparative Analysis Richard WuSchool of LawUniversity of Hong Kong 8. New Rules for Resolving Chinese Domain Name Disputes - A Comparative Analysis Richard WuSchool of LawUniversity of Hong Kong 9. Rule 2(2) CDNDRP and rules 10. CDNDRP and rules 11. "Contracting Parties to the Paris Convention". WIPO. Retrieved 2012-12-30.

12. http://www.wipo.int/treaties/en/text.jsp?file_id=288514 Paris Conventionfor the Protection of Industrial Property of March 20, 1883,as revised at Brussels on December 14, 1900,at Washington on June 2, 1911,at The Hague on November 6, 1925,at London on June 2, 1934,at Lisbon on October 31, 1958,and at Stockholm on July 14, 1967,and as amended on September 28, 1979 13. See id. 14. Alternative Dispute Resolution, An Essential Competency for Lawyers, by Mark V.B. Partridge **Oxford University Press (2009). 15.** http://www.ccpit-patent.com.cn/references/Law_Against_Unfair_Competition_China.htm law Against Unfair Competition of The People's Republic of China (Adopted at the Third Session of the Standing Committee of the Eighth National People's Congress on September 2, 1993. Promulgated by Order No. 10 of the President of the People's Republic of China on September 2, 1993. and Effective as of December 1, General Principles of THE Civil Law of the People's Republic of China (Adopted on April 12, 1986) **16, 17, & 18.** Alternative Dispute Resolution, An Essential Competency for Lawyers, by Mark V.B. Partridge **Oxford University Press (2009).**

is as easy as paying a small fee. Purchasing a domain name associated with a well-known trademark owner can be very lucrative. For the rushers who are in it for the gold, a cyber-squatter, will register a laundry list of domain names associated with 'well-known' commercial enterprises or upcoming

1. "Rushes to Statehood, The Oklahoma Land Runs". Dickinson Research Center. Retrieved 2014-05-09. **2.** Reeves, Keir; Frost, Lionel; Fahey, Charles (2010). "Integrating the Historiography of the Nineteenth-Century Gold Rushes". *Australian Economic History Review* **50** (2): 111. 3. (ICANN, 2000). **4. & 5.** Article 15 & 16 of CNDRP and rules
6. Article PRC'S Civil Procedure **7.** New Rules for Resolving Chinese Domain Name Disputes - A Comparative Analysis Richard WuSchool of LawUniversity of Hong Kong **8**. New Rules for Resolving Chinese Domain Name Disputes - A Comparative Analysis Richard WuSchool of LawUniversity of Hong Kong **9.** Rule 2(2) CDNDRP and rules **10.** CDNDRP and rules **11.** "Contracting Parties to the Paris Convention". WIPO. Retrieved 2012-12-30.

12. http://www.wipo.int/treaties/en/text.jsp?file_id=288514 Paris Conventionfor the Protection of Industrial Property of March 20, 1883,as revised at Brussels on December 14, 1900,at Washington on June 2, 1911,at The Hague on November 6, 1925,at London on June 2, 1934,at Lisbon on October 31, 1958,and at Stockholm on July 14, 1967,and as amended on September 28, 1979 **13.** See id. **14.** Alternative Dispute Resolution, An Essential Competency for Lawyers, by Mark V.B. Partridge **Oxford University Press (2009). 15.** http://www.ccpit-patent.com.cn/references/Law_Against_Unfair_Competition_China.htm law Against Unfair Competition of The People's Republic of China (Adopted at the Third Session of the Standing Committee of the Eighth National People's Congress on September 2, 1993. Promulgated by Order No. 10 of the President of the People's Republic of China on September 2, 1993. and Effective as of December 1, General Principles of THE Civil Law of the People's Republic of China (Adopted on April 12, 1986) **16, 17, & 18.** Alternative Dispute Resolution, An Essential Competency for Lawyers, by Mark V.B. Partridge **Oxford University Press (2009).**

enterprises, for a profit. The idea is to sit and wait, like literally squatting, until the enterprises offer money in order to secure the domain names for their own-gold or use the popularity to attract their consumers.

With the new era, came laws to protect the interest of

1. "Rushes to Statehood, The Oklahoma Land Runs". Dickinson Research Center. Retrieved 2014-05-09. 2. Reeves, Keir; Frost, Lionel; Fahey, Charles (2010). "Integrating the Historiography of the Nineteenth-Century Gold Rushes". *Australian Economic History Review* 50 (2): 111. 3. (ICANN, 2000). 4. & 5. Article 15 & 16 of CNDRP and rules
6. Article PRC'S Civil Procedure 7. New Rules for Resolving Chinese Domain Name Disputes - A Comparative Analysis Richard WuSchool of LawUniversity of Hong Kong 8. New Rules for Resolving Chinese Domain Name Disputes - A Comparative Analysis Richard WuSchool of LawUniversity of Hong Kong 9. Rule 2(2) CDNDRP and rules 10. CDNDRP and rules 11. "Contracting Parties to the Paris Convention". WIPO. Retrieved 2012-12-30.

12. http://www.wipo.int/treaties/en/text.jsp?file_id=288514 Paris Conventionfor the Protection of Industrial Property of March 20, 1883,as revised at Brussels on December 14, 1900,at Washington on June 2, 1911,at The Hague on November 6, 1925,at London on June 2, 1934,at Lisbon on October 31, 1958,and at Stockholm on July 14, 1967,and as amended on September 28, 1979 13. See id. 14. Alternative Dispute Resolution, An Essential Competency for Lawyers, by Mark V.B. Partridge Oxford University Press (2009). 15. http://www.ccpit-patent.com.cn/references/Law_Against_Unfair_Competition_China.htm law Against Unfair Competition of The People's Republic of China (Adopted at the Third Session of the Standing Committee of the Eighth National People's Congress on September 2, 1993. Promulgated by Order No. 10 of the President of the People's Republic of China on September 2, 1993. and Effective as of December 1, General Principles of THE Civil Law of the People's Republic of China (Adopted on April 12, 1986) 16, 17, & 18. Alternative Dispute Resolution, An Essential Competency for Lawyers, by Mark V.B. Partridge Oxford University Press (2009).

commercial enterprise electing these domain names as their intellectual property, because, like the unique name or trademark bore by the enterprise, they also maintained the right to them. The United States adopted ICANN's Uniform Domain Name Policy (UDRP) and UDRP rules for

1. "Rushes to Statehood, The Oklahoma Land Runs". Dickinson Research Center. Retrieved 2014-05-09. 2. Reeves, Keir; Frost, Lionel; Fahey, Charles (2010). "Integrating the Historiography of the Nineteenth-Century Gold Rushes". *Australian Economic History Review* 50 (2): 111. 3. (ICANN, 2000). 4. & 5. Article 15 & 16 of CNDRP and rules

6. Article PRC'S Civil Procedure 7. New Rules for Resolving Chinese Domain Name Disputes - A Comparative Analysis Richard WuSchool of LawUniversity of Hong Kong 8. New Rules for Resolving Chinese Domain Name Disputes - A Comparative Analysis Richard WuSchool of LawUniversity of Hong Kong 9. Rule 2(2) CDNDRP and rules 10. CDNDRP and rules 11. "Contracting Parties to the Paris Convention". WIPO. Retrieved 2012-12-30.

12. http://www.wipo.int/treaties/en/text.jsp?file_id=288514 Paris Conventionfor the Protection of Industrial Property of March 20, 1883,as revised at Brussels on December 14, 1900,at Washington on June 2, 1911,at The Hague on November 6, 1925,at London on June 2, 1934,at Lisbon on October 31, 1958,and at Stockholm on July 14, 1967,and as amended on September 28, 1979 13. See id. 14. Alternative Dispute Resolution, An Essential Competency for Lawyers, by Mark V.B. Partridge **Oxford University Press (2009). 15.** http://www.ccpit-patent.com.cn/references/Law_Against_Unfair_Competition_China.htm law Against Unfair Competition of The People's Republic of China (Adopted at the Third Session of the Standing Committee of the Eighth National People's Congress on September 2, 1993. Promulgated by Order No. 10 of the President of the People's Republic of China on September 2, 1993. and Effective as of December 1, General Principles of THE Civil Law of the People's Republic of China (Adopted on April 12, 1986) **16, 17, & 18.** Alternative Dispute Resolution, An Essential Competency for Lawyers, by Mark V.B. Partridge **Oxford University Press (2009).**

disputes. China, on the other hand, has the China Internet Network Information Center (CNNIC), which uses the Domain Name Dispute Resolution Center of China International Economic and Trade Arbitration Commission (CIETAC'S DNDRC) and the DNDRP and rules. These

1. "Rushes to Statehood, The Oklahoma Land Runs". Dickinson Research Center. Retrieved 2014-05-09. 2. Reeves, Keir; Frost, Lionel; Fahey, Charles (2010). "Integrating the Historiography of the Nineteenth-Century Gold Rushes". *Australian Economic History Review* 50 (2): 111. 3. (ICANN, 2000). 4. & 5. Article 15 & 16 of CNDRP and rules
6. Article PRC'S Civil Procedure 7. New Rules for Resolving Chinese Domain Name Disputes - A Comparative Analysis Richard WuSchool of LawUniversity of Hong Kong 8. New Rules for Resolving Chinese Domain Name Disputes - A Comparative Analysis Richard WuSchool of LawUniversity of Hong Kong 9. Rule 2(2) CDNDRP and rules 10. CDNDRP and rules 11. "Contracting Parties to the Paris Convention". WIPO. Retrieved 2012-12-30.

12. http://www.wipo.int/treaties/en/text.jsp?file_id=288514 Paris Conventionfor the Protection of Industrial Property of March 20, 1883,as revised at Brussels on December 14, 1900,at Washington on June 2, 1911,at The Hague on November 6, 1925,at London on June 2, 1934,at Lisbon on October 31, 1958,and at Stockholm on July 14, 1967,and as amended on September 28, 1979 13. See id. 14. Alternative Dispute Resolution, An Essential Competency for Lawyers, by Mark V.B. Partridge Oxford University Press (2009). 15. http://www.ccpit-patent.com.cn/references/Law_Against_Unfair_Competition_China.htm law Against Unfair Competition of The People's Republic of China (Adopted at the Third Session of the Standing Committee of the Eighth National People's Congress on September 2, 1993. Promulgated by Order No. 10 of the President of the People's Republic of China on September 2, 1993. and Effective as of December 1, General Principles of THE Civil Law of the People's Republic of China (Adopted on April 12, 1986) 16, 17, & 18. Alternative Dispute Resolution, An Essential Competency for Lawyers, by Mark V.B. Partridge Oxford University Press (2009).

bodies handle the overflow of disputes and, for the most part, deal with cybersquatting. Because Domain Name Disputes can be a question of trademark infringement, these cases may end up in civil court. China's Domain Name Dispute Resolution Policy is different than ICANN'S UDRP

1. "Rushes to Statehood, The Oklahoma Land Runs". Dickinson Research Center. Retrieved 2014-05-09. 2. Reeves, Keir; Frost, Lionel; Fahey, Charles (2010). "Integrating the Historiography of the Nineteenth-Century Gold Rushes". *Australian Economic History Review* 50 (2): 111. 3. (ICANN, 2000). 4. & 5. Article 15 & 16 of CNDRP and rules
6. Article PRC'S Civil Procedure 7. New Rules for Resolving Chinese Domain Name Disputes - A Comparative Analysis Richard WuSchool of LawUniversity of Hong Kong 8. New Rules for Resolving Chinese Domain Name Disputes - A Comparative Analysis Richard WuSchool of LawUniversity of Hong Kong 9. Rule 2(2) CDNDRP and rules 10. CDNDRP and rules 11. "Contracting Parties to the Paris Convention". WIPO. Retrieved 2012-12-30.

12. http://www.wipo.int/treaties/en/text.jsp?file_id=288514 Paris Conventionfor the Protection of Industrial Property of March 20, 1883,as revised at Brussels on December 14, 1900,at Washington on June 2, 1911,at The Hague on November 6, 1925,at London on June 2, 1934,at Lisbon on October 31, 1958,and at Stockholm on July 14, 1967,and as amended on September 28, 1979 13. See id. 14. Alternative Dispute Resolution, An Essential Competency for Lawyers, by Mark V.B. Partridge **Oxford University Press (2009).** 15. http://www.ccpit-patent.com.cn/references/Law_Against_Unfair_Competition_China.htm law Against Unfair Competition of The People's Republic of China (Adopted at the Third Session of the Standing Committee of the Eighth National People's Congress on September 2, 1993. Promulgated by Order No. 10 of the President of the People's Republic of China on September 2, 1993. and Effective as of December 1, General Principles of THE Civil Law of the People's Republic of China (Adopted on April 12, 1986) **16, 17, & 18.** Alternative Dispute Resolution, An Essential Competency for Lawyers, by Mark V.B. Partridge **Oxford University Press (2009).**

and rules. This article gives a strategic guide to bring a successful and proper Domain Name Dispute claim in China, and will hopefully, with use, lend in dissolving bias, which is said to exist based on cases won by trademark owners using ICANN'S UDRP and rules- 79.4% to 19.9% (3).

1. "Rushes to Statehood, The Oklahoma Land Runs". Dickinson Research Center. Retrieved 2014-05-09. **2.** Reeves, Keir; Frost, Lionel; Fahey, Charles (2010). "Integrating the Historiography of the Nineteenth-Century Gold Rushes". *Australian Economic History Review* **50** (2): 111. 3. (ICANN, 2000). **4. & 5.** Article 15 & 16 of CNDRP and rules
6. Article PRC'S Civil Procedure **7.** New Rules for Resolving Chinese Domain Name Disputes - A Comparative Analysis Richard WuSchool of LawUniversity of Hong Kong **8**. New Rules for Resolving Chinese Domain Name Disputes - A Comparative Analysis Richard WuSchool of LawUniversity of Hong Kong **9.** Rule 2(2) CDNDRP and rules **10.** CDNDRP and rules **11.** "Contracting Parties to the Paris Convention". WIPO. Retrieved 2012-12-30.

12. http://www.wipo.int/treaties/en/text.jsp?file_id=288514 Paris Conventionfor the Protection of Industrial Property of March 20, 1883,as revised at Brussels on December 14, 1900,at Washington on June 2, 1911,at The Hague on November 6, 1925,at London on June 2, 1934,at Lisbon on October 31, 1958,and at Stockholm on July 14, 1967,and as amended on September 28, 1979 **13.** See id. **14.** Alternative Dispute Resolution, An Essential Competency for Lawyers, by Mark V.B. Partridge **Oxford University Press (2009). 15.** http://www.ccpit-patent.com.cn/references/Law_Against_Unfair_Competition_China.htm law Against Unfair Competition of The People's Republic of China (Adopted at the Third Session of the Standing Committee of the Eighth National People's Congress on September 2, 1993. Promulgated by Order No. 10 of the President of the People's Republic of China on September 2, 1993. and Effective as of December 1, General Principles of THE Civil Law of the People's Republic of China (Adopted on April 12, 1986) **16, 17, & 18.** Alternative Dispute Resolution, An Essential Competency for Lawyers, by Mark V.B. Partridge **Oxford University Press (2009).**

I. Four Points Before the Dispute

First, in order for a client to bring a successful and proper complaint, they need to bring it under the right policy and rules. If the domain name was registered outside of China, then ICANN'S UDRP and

1. "Rushes to Statehood, The Oklahoma Land Runs". Dickinson Research Center. Retrieved 2014-05-09. 2. Reeves, Keir; Frost, Lionel; Fahey, Charles (2010). "Integrating the Historiography of the Nineteenth-Century Gold Rushes". *Australian Economic History Review* 50 (2): 111. 3. (ICANN, 2000). 4. & 5. Article 15 & 16 of CNDRP and rules

6. Article PRC'S Civil Procedure 7. New Rules for Resolving Chinese Domain Name Disputes - A Comparative Analysis Richard WuSchool of LawUniversity of Hong Kong 8. New Rules for Resolving Chinese Domain Name Disputes - A Comparative Analysis Richard WuSchool of LawUniversity of Hong Kong 9. Rule 2(2) CDNDRP and rules 10. CDNDRP and rules 11. "Contracting Parties to the Paris Convention". WIPO. Retrieved 2012-12-30.

12. http://www.wipo.int/treaties/en/text.jsp?file_id=288514 Paris Conventionfor the Protection of Industrial Property of March 20, 1883,as revised at Brussels on December 14, 1900,at Washington on June 2, 1911,at The Hague on November 6, 1925,at London on June 2, 1934,at Lisbon on October 31, 1958,and at Stockholm on July 14, 1967,and as amended on September 28, 1979 13. See id. 14. Alternative Dispute Resolution, An Essential Competency for Lawyers, by Mark V.B. Partridge **Oxford University Press (2009). 15.** http://www.ccpit-patent.com.cn/references/Law_Against_Unfair_Competition_China.htm law Against Unfair Competition of The People's Republic of China (Adopted at the Third Session of the Standing Committee of the Eighth National People's Congress on September 2, 1993. Promulgated by Order No. 10 of the President of the People's Republic of China on September 2, 1993. and Effective as of December 1, General Principles of THE Civil Law of the People's Republic of China (Adopted on April 12, 1986) **16, 17, & 18.** Alternative Dispute Resolution, An Essential Competency for Lawyers, by Mark V.B. Partridge **Oxford University Press (2009).**

rules apply. If the domain name was registered inside China or is claiming an unregistered name, such as a personality or famous name (4), it will fall under CANNIC'S CIETAC'S DNDRP and rules. However, any Domain Name Dispute revolving the registration of the same name cannot be heard in

1. "Rushes to Statehood, The Oklahoma Land Runs". Dickinson Research Center. Retrieved 2014-05-09. 2. Reeves, Keir; Frost, Lionel; Fahey, Charles (2010). "Integrating the Historiography of the Nineteenth-Century Gold Rushes". *Australian Economic History Review* 50 (2): 111. 3. (ICANN, 2000). 4. & 5. Article 15 & 16 of CNDRP and rules
6. Article PRC'S Civil Procedure 7. New Rules for Resolving Chinese Domain Name Disputes - A Comparative Analysis Richard WuSchool of LawUniversity of Hong Kong 8. New Rules for Resolving Chinese Domain Name Disputes - A Comparative Analysis Richard WuSchool of LawUniversity of Hong Kong 9. Rule 2(2) CDNDRP and rules 10. CDNDRP and rules 11. "Contracting Parties to the Paris Convention". WIPO. Retrieved 2012-12-30.

12. http://www.wipo.int/treaties/en/text.jsp?file_id=288514 Paris Conventionfor the Protection of Industrial Property of March 20, 1883,as revised at Brussels on December 14, 1900,at Washington on June 2, 1911,at The Hague on November 6, 1925,at London on June 2, 1934,at Lisbon on October 31, 1958,and at Stockholm on July 14, 1967,and as amended on September 28, 1979 13. See id. 14. Alternative Dispute Resolution, An Essential Competency for Lawyers, by Mark V.B. Partridge **Oxford University Press (2009)**. 15. http://www.ccpit-patent.com.cn/references/Law_Against_Unfair_Competition_China.htm law Against Unfair Competition of The People's Republic of China (Adopted at the Third Session of the Standing Committee of the Eighth National People's Congress on September 2, 1993. Promulgated by Order No. 10 of the President of the People's Republic of China on September 2, 1993. and Effective as of December 1, General Principles of THE Civil Law of the People's Republic of China (Adopted on April 12, 1986) **16, 17, & 18.** Alternative Dispute Resolution, An Essential Competency for Lawyers, by Mark V.B. Partridge **Oxford University Press (2009).**

CDNDRC. It should be brought to PRC's civil court, in the appropriate venue, and the Domain Name Registration Office (DNRO) may be held accountable in some rare circumstances, which is responsible for the physical registration of a Domain Name (5).

1. "Rushes to Statehood, The Oklahoma Land Runs". Dickinson Research Center. Retrieved 2014-05-09. 2. Reeves, Keir; Frost, Lionel; Fahey, Charles (2010). "Integrating the Historiography of the Nineteenth-Century Gold Rushes". *Australian Economic History Review* 50 (2): 111. 3. (ICANN, 2000). 4. & 5. Article 15 & 16 of CNDRP and rules
6. Article PRC'S Civil Procedure 7. New Rules for Resolving Chinese Domain Name Disputes - A Comparative Analysis Richard WuSchool of LawUniversity of Hong Kong 8. New Rules for Resolving Chinese Domain Name Disputes - A Comparative Analysis Richard WuSchool of LawUniversity of Hong Kong 9. Rule 2(2) CDNDRP and rules 10. CDNDRP and rules 11. "Contracting Parties to the Paris Convention". WIPO. Retrieved 2012-12-30.

12. http://www.wipo.int/treaties/en/text.jsp?file_id=288514 Paris Conventionfor the Protection of Industrial Property of March 20, 1883,as revised at Brussels on December 14, 1900,at Washington on June 2, 1911,at The Hague on November 6, 1925,at London on June 2, 1934,at Lisbon on October 31, 1958,and at Stockholm on July 14, 1967,and as amended on September 28, 1979 13. See id. 14. Alternative Dispute Resolution, An Essential Competency for Lawyers, by Mark V.B. Partridge **Oxford University Press (2009). 15.** http://www.ccpit-patent.com.cn/references/Law_Against_Unfair_Competition_China.htm law Against Unfair Competition of The People's Republic of China (Adopted at the Third Session of the Standing Committee of the Eighth National People's Congress on September 2, 1993. Promulgated by Order No. 10 of the President of the People's Republic of China on September 2, 1993. and Effective as of December 1, General Principles of THE Civil Law of the People's Republic of China (Adopted on April 12, 1986) **16, 17, & 18.** Alternative Dispute Resolution, An Essential Competency for Lawyers, by Mark V.B. Partridge **Oxford University Press (2009).**

Secondly, in order to bring a successful and proper claim, a client needs to appropriate their remedy. If they merely seek to cancel another parties right of a domain name or transfer it, then the CDNDRC will apply. If they seek cessation of the infringing acts and compensation, then the PRC's

1. "Rushes to Statehood, The Oklahoma Land Runs". Dickinson Research Center. Retrieved 2014-05-09. 2. Reeves, Keir; Frost, Lionel; Fahey, Charles (2010). "Integrating the Historiography of the Nineteenth-Century Gold Rushes". *Australian Economic History Review* 50 (2): 111. 3. (ICANN, 2000). 4. & 5. Article 15 & 16 of CNDRP and rules

6. Article PRC'S Civil Procedure 7. New Rules for Resolving Chinese Domain Name Disputes - A Comparative Analysis Richard WuSchool of LawUniversity of Hong Kong 8. New Rules for Resolving Chinese Domain Name Disputes - A Comparative Analysis Richard WuSchool of LawUniversity of Hong Kong 9. Rule 2(2) CDNDRP and rules 10. CDNDRP and rules 11. "Contracting Parties to the Paris Convention". WIPO. Retrieved 2012-12-30.

12. http://www.wipo.int/treaties/en/text.jsp?file_id=288514 Paris Conventionfor the Protection of Industrial Property of March 20, 1883,as revised at Brussels on December 14, 1900,at Washington on June 2, 1911,at The Hague on November 6, 1925,at London on June 2, 1934,at Lisbon on October 31, 1958,and at Stockholm on July 14, 1967,and as amended on September 28, 1979 13. See id. 14. Alternative Dispute Resolution, An Essential Competency for Lawyers, by Mark V.B. Partridge Oxford University Press (2009). 15. http://www.ccpit-patent.com.cn/references/Law_Against_Unfair_Competition_China.htm law Against Unfair Competition of The People's Republic of China (Adopted at the Third Session of the Standing Committee of the Eighth National People's Congress on September 2, 1993. Promulgated by Order No. 10 of the President of the People's Republic of China on September 2, 1993. and Effective as of December 1, General Principles of THE Civil Law of the People's Republic of China (Adopted on April 12, 1986) 16, 17, & 18. Alternative Dispute Resolution, An Essential Competency for Lawyers, by Mark V.B. Partridge Oxford University Press (2009).

civil court will apply. However, it is possible to bring a claim through the CNDRC, and if they are not happy with the result or for whatever reason, they may bring the same case within ten calendar days to the PRC's civil court (4, 5). And from there, they may appeal or remove to the PRC's higher

1. "Rushes to Statehood, The Oklahoma Land Runs". Dickinson Research Center. Retrieved 2014-05-09. 2. Reeves, Keir; Frost, Lionel; Fahey, Charles (2010). "Integrating the Historiography of the Nineteenth-Century Gold Rushes". *Australian Economic History Review* 50 (2): 111. 3. (ICANN, 2000). 4. & 5. Article 15 & 16 of CNDRP and rules
6. Article PRC'S Civil Procedure 7. New Rules for Resolving Chinese Domain Name Disputes - A Comparative Analysis Richard WuSchool of LawUniversity of Hong Kong 8. New Rules for Resolving Chinese Domain Name Disputes - A Comparative Analysis Richard WuSchool of LawUniversity of Hong Kong 9. Rule 2(2) CDNDRP and rules 10. CDNDRP and rules 11. "Contracting Parties to the Paris Convention". WIPO. Retrieved 2012-12-30.

12. http://www.wipo.int/treaties/en/text.jsp?file_id=288514 Paris Conventionfor the Protection of Industrial Property of March 20, 1883,as revised at Brussels on December 14, 1900,at Washington on June 2, 1911,at The Hague on November 6, 1925,at London on June 2, 1934,at Lisbon on October 31, 1958,and at Stockholm on July 14, 1967,and as amended on September 28, 1979 13. See id. 14. Alternative Dispute Resolution, An Essential Competency for Lawyers, by Mark V.B. Partridge **Oxford University Press (2009).** 15. http://www.ccpit-patent.com.cn/references/Law_Against_Unfair_Competition_China.htm law Against Unfair Competition of The People's Republic of China (Adopted at the Third Session of the Standing Committee of the Eighth National People's Congress on September 2, 1993. Promulgated by Order No. 10 of the President of the People's Republic of China on September 2, 1993. and Effective as of December 1, General Principles of THE Civil Law of the People's Republic of China (Adopted on April 12, 1986) **16, 17, & 18.** Alternative Dispute Resolution, An Essential Competency for Lawyers, by Mark V.B. Partridge **Oxford University Press (2009).**

court (6), and then, may petition to the PRC's Supreme Court. However, all judicial decisions prevail over the CDNDRC's decision (7).

Thirdly, before bringing a claim, a client must understand the costs for bringing a Domain Name Dispute in China for each situation and

1. "Rushes to Statehood, The Oklahoma Land Runs". Dickinson Research Center. Retrieved 2014-05-09. **2.** Reeves, Keir; Frost, Lionel; Fahey, Charles (2010). "Integrating the Historiography of the Nineteenth-Century Gold Rushes". *Australian Economic History Review* **50** (2): 111. 3. (ICANN, 2000). **4. & 5.** Article 15 & 16 of CNDRP and rules

6. Article PRC'S Civil Procedure **7.** New Rules for Resolving Chinese Domain Name Disputes - A Comparative Analysis Richard WuSchool of LawUniversity of Hong Kong **8.** New Rules for Resolving Chinese Domain Name Disputes - A Comparative Analysis Richard WuSchool of LawUniversity of Hong Kong **9.** Rule 2(2) CDNDRP and rules **10.** CDNDRP and rules **11.** "Contracting Parties to the Paris Convention". WIPO. Retrieved 2012-12-30.

12. http://www.wipo.int/treaties/en/text.jsp?file_id=288514 Paris Conventionfor the Protection of Industrial Property of March 20, 1883,as revised at Brussels on December 14, 1900,at Washington on June 2, 1911,at The Hague on November 6, 1925,at London on June 2, 1934,at Lisbon on October 31, 1958,and at Stockholm on July 14, 1967,and as amended on September 28, 1979 **13.** See id. **14.** Alternative Dispute Resolution, An Essential Competency for Lawyers, by Mark V.B. Partridge **Oxford University Press (2009). 15.** http://www.ccpit-patent.com.cn/references/Law_Against_Unfair_Competition_China.htm law Against Unfair Competition of The People's Republic of China (Adopted at the Third Session of the Standing Committee of the Eighth National People's Congress on September 2, 1993. Promulgated by Order No. 10 of the President of the People's Republic of China on September 2, 1993. and Effective as of December 1, General Principles of THE Civil Law of the People's Republic of China (Adopted on April 12, 1986) **16, 17, & 18.** Alternative Dispute Resolution, An Essential Competency for Lawyers, by Mark V.B. Partridge **Oxford University Press (2009).**

circumstance. For instance, a dispute in civil court involves costly litigation, China's DNDRC is cheaper, paying the cyber-squatter's nuisance value (8) may be cheaper, and registering the domain name before someone else is the cheapest alternative, if applicable. Keeping in mind,

1. "Rushes to Statehood, The Oklahoma Land Runs". Dickinson Research Center. Retrieved 2014-05-09. 2. Reeves, Keir; Frost, Lionel; Fahey, Charles (2010). "Integrating the Historiography of the Nineteenth-Century Gold Rushes". *Australian Economic History Review* 50 (2): 111. 3. (ICANN, 2000). 4. & 5. Article 15 & 16 of CNDRP and rules

6. Article PRC'S Civil Procedure 7. New Rules for Resolving Chinese Domain Name Disputes - A Comparative Analysis Richard WuSchool of LawUniversity of Hong Kong 8. New Rules for Resolving Chinese Domain Name Disputes - A Comparative Analysis Richard WuSchool of LawUniversity of Hong Kong 9. Rule 2(2) CDNDRP and rules 10. CDNDRP and rules 11. "Contracting Parties to the Paris Convention". WIPO. Retrieved 2012-12-30.

12. http://www.wipo.int/treaties/en/text.jsp?file_id=288514 Paris Conventionfor the Protection of Industrial Property of March 20, 1883,as revised at Brussels on December 14, 1900,at Washington on June 2, 1911,at The Hague on November 6, 1925,at London on June 2, 1934,at Lisbon on October 31, 1958,and at Stockholm on July 14, 1967,and as amended on September 28, 1979 13. See id. 14. Alternative Dispute Resolution, An Essential Competency for Lawyers, by Mark V.B. Partridge **Oxford University Press (2009). 15.** http://www.ccpit-patent.com.cn/references/Law_Against_Unfair_Competition_China.htm law Against Unfair Competition of The People's Republic of China (Adopted at the Third Session of the Standing Committee of the Eighth National People's Congress on September 2, 1993. Promulgated by Order No. 10 of the President of the People's Republic of China on September 2, 1993. and Effective as of December 1, General Principles of THE Civil Law of the People's Republic of China (Adopted on April 12, 1986) **16, 17, & 18.** Alternative Dispute Resolution, An Essential Competency for Lawyers, by Mark V.B. Partridge **Oxford University Press (2009).**

the longer the domain dispute lasts, the larger the losses the trademark owner will suffer, considering they are a commercial enterprise and their site brings in low to high revenue.

And lastly, in order to bring a successful and proper claim, a client must be aware of the

1. "Rushes to Statehood, The Oklahoma Land Runs". Dickinson Research Center. Retrieved 2014-05-09. **2.** Reeves, Keir; Frost, Lionel; Fahey, Charles (2010). "Integrating the Historiography of the Nineteenth-Century Gold Rushes". *Australian Economic History Review* **50** (2): 111. 3. (ICANN, 2000). **4. & 5.** Article 15 & 16 of CNDRP and rules
6. Article PRC'S Civil Procedure **7.** New Rules for Resolving Chinese Domain Name Disputes - A Comparative Analysis Richard WuSchool of LawUniversity of Hong Kong **8.** New Rules for Resolving Chinese Domain Name Disputes - A Comparative Analysis Richard WuSchool of LawUniversity of Hong Kong **9.** Rule 2(2) CDNDRP and rules **10.** CDNDRP and rules **11.** "Contracting Parties to the Paris Convention". WIPO. Retrieved 2012-12-30.

12. http://www.wipo.int/treaties/en/text.jsp?file_id=288514 Paris Conventionfor the Protection of Industrial Property of March 20, 1883,as revised at Brussels on December 14, 1900,at Washington on June 2, 1911,at The Hague on November 6, 1925,at London on June 2, 1934,at Lisbon on October 31, 1958,and at Stockholm on July 14, 1967,and as amended on September 28, 1979 **13.** See id. **14.** Alternative Dispute Resolution, An Essential Competency for Lawyers, by Mark V.B. Partridge **Oxford University Press (2009). 15.** http://www.ccpit-patent.com.cn/references/Law_Against_Unfair_Competition_China.htm law Against Unfair Competition of The People's Republic of China (Adopted at the Third Session of the Standing Committee of the Eighth National People's Congress on September 2, 1993. Promulgated by Order No. 10 of the President of the People's Republic of China on September 2, 1993. and Effective as of December 1, General Principles of THE Civil Law of the People's Republic of China (Adopted on April 12, 1986) **16, 17, & 18.** Alternative Dispute Resolution, An Essential Competency for Lawyers, by Mark V.B. Partridge **Oxford University Press (2009).**

statute of limitations, which is unique to China's DNDRP and rules. Unlike ICANN's UDRP and rules, the CDNDRP limits each domain dispute to two years before the implication of the policy, 2000, and two years after the discovered infringement or registry (9).

1. "Rushes to Statehood, The Oklahoma Land Runs". Dickinson Research Center. Retrieved 2014-05-09. 2. Reeves, Keir; Frost, Lionel; Fahey, Charles (2010). "Integrating the Historiography of the Nineteenth-Century Gold Rushes". *Australian Economic History Review* 50 (2): 111. 3. (ICANN, 2000). 4. & 5. Article 15 & 16 of CNDRP and rules
6. Article PRC'S Civil Procedure 7. New Rules for Resolving Chinese Domain Name Disputes - A Comparative Analysis Richard WuSchool of LawUniversity of Hong Kong 8. New Rules for Resolving Chinese Domain Name Disputes - A Comparative Analysis Richard WuSchool of LawUniversity of Hong Kong 9. Rule 2(2) CDNDRP and rules 10. CDNDRP and rules 11. "Contracting Parties to the Paris Convention". WIPO. Retrieved 2012-12-30.

12. http://www.wipo.int/treaties/en/text.jsp?file_id=288514 Paris Conventionfor the Protection of Industrial Property of March 20, 1883,as revised at Brussels on December 14, 1900,at Washington on June 2, 1911,at The Hague on November 6, 1925,at London on June 2, 1934,at Lisbon on October 31, 1958,and at Stockholm on July 14, 1967,and as amended on September 28, 1979 13. See id. 14. Alternative Dispute Resolution, An Essential Competency for Lawyers, by Mark V.B. Partridge **Oxford University Press (2009). 15.** http://www.ccpit-patent.com.cn/references/Law_Against_Unfair_Competition_China.htm law Against Unfair Competition of The People's Republic of China (Adopted at the Third Session of the Standing Committee of the Eighth National People's Congress on September 2, 1993. Promulgated by Order No. 10 of the President of the People's Republic of China on September 2, 1993. and Effective as of December 1, General Principles of THE Civil Law of the People's Republic of China (Adopted on April 12, 1986) **16, 17, & 18.** Alternative Dispute Resolution, An Essential Competency for Lawyers, by Mark V.B. Partridge **Oxford University Press (2009).**

II. The Four Factors of a Dispute

The CDNDRC was created to ensure the fairness, convenience, and expeditiousness of domain dispute resolution procedures. The CDNDRP and rules etch out five factors that are considered one-by-one by the

1. "Rushes to Statehood, The Oklahoma Land Runs". Dickinson Research Center. Retrieved 2014-05-09. **2.** Reeves, Keir; Frost, Lionel; Fahey, Charles (2010). "Integrating the Historiography of the Nineteenth-Century Gold Rushes". *Australian Economic History Review* **50** (2): 111. 3. (ICANN, 2000). **4. & 5.** Article 15 & 16 of CNDRP and rules
6. Article PRC'S Civil Procedure **7.** New Rules for Resolving Chinese Domain Name Disputes - A Comparative Analysis Richard WuSchool of LawUniversity of Hong Kong **8.** New Rules for Resolving Chinese Domain Name Disputes - A Comparative Analysis Richard WuSchool of LawUniversity of Hong Kong **9.** Rule 2(2) CDNDRP and rules **10.** CDNDRP and rules **11.** "Contracting Parties to the Paris Convention". WIPO. Retrieved 2012-12-30.

12. http://www.wipo.int/treaties/en/text.jsp?file_id=288514 Paris Conventionfor the Protection of Industrial Property of March 20, 1883,as revised at Brussels on December 14, 1900,at Washington on June 2, 1911,at The Hague on November 6, 1925,at London on June 2, 1934,at Lisbon on October 31, 1958,and at Stockholm on July 14, 1967,and as amended on September 28, 1979 **13.** See id. **14.** Alternative Dispute Resolution, An Essential Competency for Lawyers, by Mark V.B. Partridge **Oxford University Press (2009).** **15.** http://www.ccpit-patent.com.cn/references/Law_Against_Unfair_Competition_China.htm law Against Unfair Competition of The People's Republic of China (Adopted at the Third Session of the Standing Committee of the Eighth National People's Congress on September 2, 1993. Promulgated by Order No. 10 of the President of the People's Republic of China on September 2, 1993. and Effective as of December 1, General Principles of THE Civil Law of the People's Republic of China (Adopted on April 12, 1986) **16, 17, & 18.** Alternative Dispute Resolution, An Essential Competency for Lawyers, by Mark V.B. Partridge **Oxford University Press (2009).**

CDNDRC's panelist, when validating a claim or defense (10):

1. 'Identical or Confusingly Similar'
The Paris Convention, which was signed in Paris, France on 20 March 1883 (11). Article 2 and 3 of the Paris

1. "Rushes to Statehood, The Oklahoma Land Runs". Dickinson Research Center. Retrieved 2014-05-09. **2.** Reeves, Keir; Frost, Lionel; Fahey, Charles (2010). "Integrating the Historiography of the Nineteenth-Century Gold Rushes". *Australian Economic History Review* **50** (2): 111. **3.** (ICANN, 2000). **4. & 5.** Article 15 & 16 of CNDRP and rules
6. Article PRC'S Civil Procedure **7.** New Rules for Resolving Chinese Domain Name Disputes - A Comparative Analysis Richard WuSchool of LawUniversity of Hong Kong **8.** New Rules for Resolving Chinese Domain Name Disputes - A Comparative Analysis Richard WuSchool of LawUniversity of Hong Kong **9.** Rule 2(2) CDNDRP and rules **10.** CDNDRP and rules **11.** "Contracting Parties to the Paris Convention". WIPO. Retrieved 2012-12-30.

12. http://www.wipo.int/treaties/en/text.jsp?file_id=288514 Paris Conventionfor the Protection of Industrial Property of March 20, 1883,as revised at Brussels on December 14, 1900,at Washington on June 2, 1911,at The Hague on November 6, 1925,at London on June 2, 1934,at Lisbon on October 31, 1958,and at Stockholm on July 14, 1967,and as amended on September 28, 1979 **13.** See id. **14.** Alternative Dispute Resolution, An Essential Competency for Lawyers, by Mark V.B. Partridge **Oxford University Press (2009). 15.** http://www.ccpit-patent.com.cn/references/Law_Against_Unfair_Competition_China.htm law Against Unfair Competition of The People's Republic of China (Adopted at the Third Session of the Standing Committee of the Eighth National People's Congress on September 2, 1993. Promulgated by Order No. 10 of the President of the People's Republic of China on September 2, 1993. and Effective as of December 1, General Principles of THE Civil Law of the People's Republic of China (Adopted on April 12, 1986) **16, 17, & 18.** Alternative Dispute Resolution, An Essential Competency for Lawyers, by Mark V.B. Partridge **Oxford University Press (2009).**

Convention for the Protection of Industrial Property states in parts: "Anyone either national or domiciled in a state party of the convention shall enjoy in all other countries of the union, the advantages that their respective law grants to nationals" (12). When a client registers their trademark in a

1. "Rushes to Statehood, The Oklahoma Land Runs". Dickinson Research Center. Retrieved 2014-05-09. 2. Reeves, Keir; Frost, Lionel; Fahey, Charles (2010). "Integrating the Historiography of the Nineteenth-Century Gold Rushes". *Australian Economic History Review* 50 (2): 111. 3. (ICANN, 2000). 4. & 5. Article 15 & 16 of CNDRP and rules
6. Article PRC'S Civil Procedure 7. New Rules for Resolving Chinese Domain Name Disputes - A Comparative Analysis Richard WuSchool of LawUniversity of Hong Kong 8. New Rules for Resolving Chinese Domain Name Disputes - A Comparative Analysis Richard WuSchool of LawUniversity of Hong Kong 9. Rule 2(2) CDNDRP and rules 10. CDNDRP and rules 11. "Contracting Parties to the Paris Convention". WIPO. Retrieved 2012-12-30.

12. http://www.wipo.int/treaties/en/text.jsp?file_id=288514 Paris Conventionfor the Protection of Industrial Property of March 20, 1883,as revised at Brussels on December 14, 1900,at Washington on June 2, 1911,at The Hague on November 6, 1925,at London on June 2, 1934,at Lisbon on October 31, 1958,and at Stockholm on July 14, 1967,and as amended on September 28, 1979 13. See id. 14. Alternative Dispute Resolution, An Essential Competency for Lawyers, by Mark V.B. Partridge **Oxford University Press (2009). 15.** http://www.ccpit-patent.com.cn/references/Law_Against_Unfair_Competition_China.htm law Against Unfair Competition of The People's Republic of China (Adopted at the Third Session of the Standing Committee of the Eighth National People's Congress on September 2, 1993. Promulgated by Order No. 10 of the President of the People's Republic of China on September 2, 1993. and Effective as of December 1, General Principles of THE Civil Law of the People's Republic of China (Adopted on April 12, 1986) **16, 17, & 18.** Alternative Dispute Resolution, An Essential Competency for Lawyers, by Mark V.B. Partridge **Oxford University Press (2009).**

foreign country that is a member of this union, the client receives the same treatment as if it came from a national of that foreign country. The client shall benefit from the same protection and same legal remedy against any infringement on their domain name, as if they were a national

1. "Rushes to Statehood, The Oklahoma Land Runs". Dickinson Research Center. Retrieved 2014-05-09. 2. Reeves, Keir; Frost, Lionel; Fahey, Charles (2010). "Integrating the Historiography of the Nineteenth-Century Gold Rushes". *Australian Economic History Review* **50** (2): 111. 3. (ICANN, 2000). **4. & 5.** Article 15 & 16 of CNDRP and rules
6. Article PRC'S Civil Procedure 7. New Rules for Resolving Chinese Domain Name Disputes - A Comparative Analysis Richard WuSchool of LawUniversity of Hong Kong 8. New Rules for Resolving Chinese Domain Name Disputes - A Comparative Analysis Richard WuSchool of LawUniversity of Hong Kong 9. Rule 2(2) CDNDRP and rules 10. CDNDRP and rules 11. "Contracting Parties to the Paris Convention". WIPO. Retrieved 2012-12-30.

12. http://www.wipo.int/treaties/en/text.jsp?file_id=288514 Paris Conventionfor the Protection of Industrial Property of March 20, 1883,as revised at Brussels on December 14, 1900,at Washington on June 2, 1911,at The Hague on November 6, 1925,at London on June 2, 1934,at Lisbon on October 31, 1958,and at Stockholm on July 14, 1967,and as amended on September 28, 1979 **13.** See id. **14.** Alternative Dispute Resolution, An Essential Competency for Lawyers, by Mark V.B. Partridge **Oxford University Press (2009). 15.** http://www.ccpit-patent.com.cn/references/Law_Against_Unfair_Competition_China.htm law Against Unfair Competition of The People's Republic of China (Adopted at the Third Session of the Standing Committee of the Eighth National People's Congress on September 2, 1993. Promulgated by Order No. 10 of the President of the People's Republic of China on September 2, 1993. and Effective as of December 1, General Principles of THE Civil Law of the People's Republic of China (Adopted on April 12, 1986) **16, 17, & 18.** Alternative Dispute Resolution, An Essential Competency for Lawyers, by Mark V.B. Partridge **Oxford University Press (2009).**

in the country where it had been infringed upon. If the domain name is identical or confusingly similar to the trademark, then the client has a right to cancel, transfer, or in some cases seek damages.
In <u>Procter & Gamble Company v. Beijing Guowang Information Co., Ltd.</u>, a claim

1. "Rushes to Statehood, The Oklahoma Land Runs". Dickinson Research Center. Retrieved 2014-05-09. 2. Reeves, Keir; Frost, Lionel; Fahey, Charles (2010). "Integrating the Historiography of the Nineteenth-Century Gold Rushes". *Australian Economic History Review* 50 (2): 111. 3. (ICANN, 2000). 4. & 5. Article 15 & 16 of CNDRP and rules
6. Article PRC'S Civil Procedure 7. New Rules for Resolving Chinese Domain Name Disputes - A Comparative Analysis Richard WuSchool of LawUniversity of Hong Kong 8. New Rules for Resolving Chinese Domain Name Disputes - A Comparative Analysis Richard WuSchool of LawUniversity of Hong Kong 9. Rule 2(2) CDNDRP and rules 10. CDNDRP and rules 11. "Contracting Parties to the Paris Convention". WIPO. Retrieved 2012-12-30.

12. http://www.wipo.int/treaties/en/text.jsp?file_id=288514 Paris Conventionfor the Protection of Industrial Property of March 20, 1883,as revised at Brussels on December 14, 1900,at Washington on June 2, 1911,at The Hague on November 6, 1925,at London on June 2, 1934,at Lisbon on October 31, 1958,and at Stockholm on July 14, 1967,and as amended on September 28, 1979 13. See id. 14. Alternative Dispute Resolution, An Essential Competency for Lawyers, by Mark V.B. Partridge **Oxford University Press (2009)**. 15. http://www.ccpit-patent.com.cn/references/Law_Against_Unfair_Competition_China.htm law Against Unfair Competition of The People's Republic of China (Adopted at the Third Session of the Standing Committee of the Eighth National People's Congress on September 2, 1993. Promulgated by Order No. 10 of the President of the People's Republic of China on September 2, 1993. and Effective as of December 1, General Principles of THE Civil Law of the People's Republic of China (Adopted on April 12, 1986) **16, 17, & 18**. Alternative Dispute Resolution, An Essential Competency for Lawyers, by Mark V.B. Partridge **Oxford University Press (2009)**.

was filed with the PRC's civil court because of a similarity between the trademark IKEA and the domain name ITEA.com.cn. The complainant argued, through a direct comparison, their pronunciations, appearances, letter orders, and the way the consumers used the name were

1. "Rushes to Statehood, The Oklahoma Land Runs". Dickinson Research Center. Retrieved 2014-05-09. 2. Reeves, Keir; Frost, Lionel; Fahey, Charles (2010). "Integrating the Historiography of the Nineteenth-Century Gold Rushes". *Australian Economic History Review* 50 (2): 111. 3. (ICANN, 2000). 4. & 5. Article 15 & 16 of CNDRP and rules

6. Article PRC'S Civil Procedure 7. New Rules for Resolving Chinese Domain Name Disputes - A Comparative Analysis Richard WuSchool of LawUniversity of Hong Kong 8. New Rules for Resolving Chinese Domain Name Disputes - A Comparative Analysis Richard WuSchool of LawUniversity of Hong Kong 9. Rule 2(2) CDNDRP and rules 10. CDNDRP and rules 11. "Contracting Parties to the Paris Convention". WIPO. Retrieved 2012-12-30.

12. http://www.wipo.int/treaties/en/text.jsp?file_id=288514 Paris Conventionfor the Protection of Industrial Property of March 20, 1883,as revised at Brussels on December 14, 1900,at Washington on June 2, 1911,at The Hague on November 6, 1925,at London on June 2, 1934,at Lisbon on October 31, 1958,and at Stockholm on July 14, 1967,and as amended on September 28, 1979 13. See id. 14. Alternative Dispute Resolution, An Essential Competency for Lawyers, by Mark V.B. Partridge **Oxford University Press (2009). 15.** http://www.ccpit-patent.com.cn/references/Law_Against_Unfair_Competition_China.htm law Against Unfair Competition of The People's Republic of China (Adopted at the Third Session of the Standing Committee of the Eighth National People's Congress on September 2, 1993. Promulgated by Order No. 10 of the President of the People's Republic of China on September 2, 1993. and Effective as of December 1, General Principles of THE Civil Law of the People's Republic of China (Adopted on April 12, 1986) **16, 17, & 18.** Alternative Dispute Resolution, An Essential Competency for Lawyers, by Mark V.B. Partridge **Oxford University Press (2009).**

exactly the same. The respondent argued the 'i' represented Internet and 'kea' was the dictionary term for parrot, which validated the voicemail system they were preparing to launch. The court held the domain name 'ikea' was 'confusingly similar', because of the uniqueness of

1. "Rushes to Statehood, The Oklahoma Land Runs". Dickinson Research Center. Retrieved 2014-05-09. 2. Reeves, Keir; Frost, Lionel; Fahey, Charles (2010). "Integrating the Historiography of the Nineteenth-Century Gold Rushes". *Australian Economic History Review* 50 (2): 111. 3. (ICANN, 2000). 4. & 5. Article 15 & 16 of CNDRP and rules

6. Article PRC'S Civil Procedure 7. New Rules for Resolving Chinese Domain Name Disputes - A Comparative Analysis Richard WuSchool of LawUniversity of Hong Kong 8. New Rules for Resolving Chinese Domain Name Disputes - A Comparative Analysis Richard WuSchool of LawUniversity of Hong Kong 9. Rule 2(2) CDNDRP and rules 10. CDNDRP and rules 11. "Contracting Parties to the Paris Convention". WIPO. Retrieved 2012-12-30.

12. http://www.wipo.int/treaties/en/text.jsp?file_id=288514 Paris Conventionfor the Protection of Industrial Property of March 20, 1883,as revised at Brussels on December 14, 1900,at Washington on June 2, 1911,at The Hague on November 6, 1925,at London on June 2, 1934,at Lisbon on October 31, 1958,and at Stockholm on July 14, 1967,and as amended on September 28, 1979 13. See id. 14. Alternative Dispute Resolution, An Essential Competency for Lawyers, by Mark V.B. Partridge **Oxford University Press (2009).** 15. http://www.ccpit-patent.com.cn/references/Law_Against_Unfair_Competition_China.htm law Against Unfair Competition of The People's Republic of China (Adopted at the Third Session of the Standing Committee of the Eighth National People's Congress on September 2, 1993. Promulgated by Order No. 10 of the President of the People's Republic of China on September 2, 1993. and Effective as of December 1, General Principles of THE Civil Law of the People's Republic of China (Adopted on April 12, 1986) **16, 17, & 18.** Alternative Dispute Resolution, An Essential Competency for Lawyers, by Mark V.B. Partridge **Oxford University Press (2009).**

the 'well-known' trademark misleading consumers.

However in <u>Mercer Human Resource Consulting, Inc. v. Meyth International Consulting Co., Ltd.</u>, a claim was filed with the CDNDRC because of a similarity between the trademark Mercer and the domain name mercer.com.cn.

1. "Rushes to Statehood, The Oklahoma Land Runs". Dickinson Research Center. Retrieved 2014-05-09. 2. Reeves, Keir; Frost, Lionel; Fahey, Charles (2010). "Integrating the Historiography of the Nineteenth-Century Gold Rushes". *Australian Economic History Review* 50 (2): 111. 3. (ICANN, 2000). 4. & 5. Article 15 & 16 of CNDRP and rules
6. Article PRC'S Civil Procedure 7. New Rules for Resolving Chinese Domain Name Disputes - A Comparative Analysis Richard WuSchool of LawUniversity of Hong Kong 8. New Rules for Resolving Chinese Domain Name Disputes - A Comparative Analysis Richard WuSchool of LawUniversity of Hong Kong 9. Rule 2(2) CDNDRP and rules 10. CDNDRP and rules 11. "Contracting Parties to the Paris Convention". WIPO. Retrieved 2012-12-30.

12. http://www.wipo.int/treaties/en/text.jsp?file_id=288514 Paris Conventionfor the Protection of Industrial Property of March 20, 1883,as revised at Brussels on December 14, 1900,at Washington on June 2, 1911,at The Hague on November 6, 1925,at London on June 2, 1934,at Lisbon on October 31, 1958,and at Stockholm on July 14, 1967,and as amended on September 28, 1979 13. See id. 14. Alternative Dispute Resolution, An Essential Competency for Lawyers, by Mark V.B. Partridge Oxford University Press (2009). 15. http://www.ccpit-patent.com.cn/references/Law_Against_Unfair_Competition_China.htm law Against Unfair Competition of The People's Republic of China (Adopted at the Third Session of the Standing Committee of the Eighth National People's Congress on September 2, 1993. Promulgated by Order No. 10 of the President of the People's Republic of China on September 2, 1993. and Effective as of December 1, General Principles of THE Civil Law of the People's Republic of China (Adopted on April 12, 1986) 16, 17, & 18. Alternative Dispute Resolution, An Essential Competency for Lawyers, by Mark V.B. Partridge Oxford University Press (2009).

The respondent argued that the English word Mercer is not approved by Chinese law, and that the actual trademark is 'mi-shi' in Chinese, according to the dictionary, therefore they are not 'confusingly similar'. The CNDRC, Beijing Higher People's Court, and Supreme People's Court found no merit

1. "Rushes to Statehood, The Oklahoma Land Runs". Dickinson Research Center. Retrieved 2014-05-09. 2. Reeves, Keir; Frost, Lionel; Fahey, Charles (2010). "Integrating the Historiography of the Nineteenth-Century Gold Rushes". *Australian Economic History Review* 50 (2): 111. 3. (ICANN, 2000). 4. & 5. Article 15 & 16 of CNDRP and rules
6. Article PRC'S Civil Procedure 7. New Rules for Resolving Chinese Domain Name Disputes - A Comparative Analysis Richard WuSchool of LawUniversity of Hong Kong 8. New Rules for Resolving Chinese Domain Name Disputes - A Comparative Analysis Richard WuSchool of LawUniversity of Hong Kong 9. Rule 2(2) CDNDRP and rules 10. CDNDRP and rules 11. "Contracting Parties to the Paris Convention". WIPO. Retrieved 2012-12-30.

12. http://www.wipo.int/treaties/en/text.jsp?file_id=288514 Paris Conventionfor the Protection of Industrial Property of March 20, 1883,as revised at Brussels on December 14, 1900,at Washington on June 2, 1911,at The Hague on November 6, 1925,at London on June 2, 1934,at Lisbon on October 31, 1958,and at Stockholm on July 14, 1967,and as amended on September 28, 1979 13. See id. 14. Alternative Dispute Resolution, An Essential Competency for Lawyers, by Mark V.B. Partridge **Oxford University Press (2009). 15.** http://www.ccpit-patent.com.cn/references/Law_Against_Unfair_Competition_China.htm law Against Unfair Competition of The People's Republic of China (Adopted at the Third Session of the Standing Committee of the Eighth National People's Congress on September 2, 1993. Promulgated by Order No. 10 of the President of the People's Republic of China on September 2, 1993. and Effective as of December 1, General Principles of THE Civil Law of the People's Republic of China (Adopted on April 12, 1986) **16, 17, & 18.** Alternative Dispute Resolution, An Essential Competency for Lawyers, by Mark V.B. Partridge **Oxford University Press (2009).**

in this defense, and the domain name was found to be 'confusingly similar' to the trademark.

And in <u>Procter & Gamble Company v. Shnhai Chenxuan Technology and Trade Co. Ltd</u>, a claim was filed with the CDNDRC because of a similarity between the

1. "Rushes to Statehood, The Oklahoma Land Runs". Dickinson Research Center. Retrieved 2014-05-09. **2.** Reeves, Keir; Frost, Lionel; Fahey, Charles (2010). "Integrating the Historiography of the Nineteenth-Century Gold Rushes". *Australian Economic History Review* **50** (2): 111. 3. (<u>ICANN, 2000</u>). **4. & 5.** Article 15 & 16 of CNDRP and rules

6. Article PRC'S Civil Procedure **7.** New Rules for Resolving Chinese Domain Name Disputes - A Comparative Analysis Richard WuSchool of LawUniversity of Hong Kong **8**. New Rules for Resolving Chinese Domain Name Disputes - A Comparative Analysis Richard WuSchool of LawUniversity of Hong Kong **9.** Rule 2(2) CDNDRP and rules **10.** CDNDRP and rules **11.** "Contracting Parties to the Paris Convention". WIPO. Retrieved 2012-12-30.

12. <u>http://www.wipo.int/treaties/en/text.jsp?file_id=288514</u> Paris Conventionfor the Protection of Industrial Property of March 20, 1883,as revised at Brussels on December 14, 1900,at Washington on June 2, 1911,at The Hague on November 6, 1925,at London on June 2, 1934,at Lisbon on

October 31, 1958,and at Stockholm on July 14, 1967,and as amended on September 28, 1979 **13.** See id. **14.** Alternative Dispute Resolution, An Essential Competency for Lawyers, by Mark V.B. Partridge **Oxford University Press (2009). 15.** <u>http://www.ccpit-patent.com.cn/references/Law_Against_Unfair_Competition_China.htm</u> law Against Unfair Competition of The People's Republic of China (Adopted at the Third Session of the Standing Committee of the Eighth National People's Congress on September 2, 1993. Promulgated by Order No.

10 of the President of the People's Republic of China on September 2, 1993. and Effective as of December 1, General Principles of THE Civil Law of the People's Republic of China (Adopted on April 12, 1986) **16, 17, & 18.** Alternative Dispute Resolution, An Essential Competency for Lawyers, by Mark V.B. Partridge **Oxford University Press (2009).**

trademark SAFEGUARD and the domain name safeguard.com.cn. The respondent received a cease and disease letter from P&G, and then re-registered the domain name under a different company name, claiming the meaning "safeguard" to "guard and protect" fits their business

1. "Rushes to Statehood, The Oklahoma Land Runs". Dickinson Research Center. Retrieved 2014-05-09. **2.** Reeves, Keir; Frost, Lionel; Fahey, Charles (2010). "Integrating the Historiography of the Nineteenth-Century Gold Rushes". *Australian Economic History Review* **50** (2): 111. 3. (ICANN, 2000). **4. & 5.** Article 15 & 16 of CNDRP and rules
6. Article PRC'S Civil Procedure **7.** New Rules for Resolving Chinese Domain Name Disputes - A Comparative Analysis Richard WuSchool of LawUniversity of Hong Kong **8**. New Rules for Resolving Chinese Domain Name Disputes - A Comparative Analysis Richard WuSchool of LawUniversity of Hong Kong **9.** Rule 2(2) CDNDRP and rules **10.** CDNDRP and rules **11.** "Contracting Parties to the Paris Convention". WIPO. Retrieved 2012-12-30.

12. http://www.wipo.int/treaties/en/text.jsp?file_id=288514 Paris Conventionfor the Protection of Industrial Property of March 20, 1883,as revised at Brussels on December 14, 1900,at Washington on June 2, 1911,at The Hague on November 6, 1925,at London on June 2, 1934,at Lisbon on October 31, 1958,and at Stockholm on July 14, 1967,and as amended on September 28, 1979 **13.** See id. **14.** Alternative Dispute Resolution, An Essential Competency for Lawyers, by Mark V.B. Partridge **Oxford University Press (2009). 15.** http://www.ccpit-patent.com.cn/references/Law_Against_Unfair_Competition_China.htm law Against Unfair Competition of The People's Republic of China (Adopted at the Third Session of the Standing Committee of the Eighth National People's Congress on September 2, 1993. Promulgated by Order No. 10 of the President of the People's Republic of China on September 2, 1993. and Effective as of December 1, General Principles of THE Civil Law of the People's Republic of China (Adopted on April 12, 1986) **16, 17, & 18.** Alternative Dispute Resolution, An Essential Competency for Lawyers, by Mark V.B. Partridge **Oxford University Press (2009).**

plan. The CNDRC and court found no merit in this defense, and the domain name was found to be 'confusingly similar' to the trademark.

However in <u>Madonna Ciccone, v. Dan Parisi</u>, a claim was filed with the ICANN because of a similarity between the personality and famous

1. "Rushes to Statehood, The Oklahoma Land Runs". Dickinson Research Center. Retrieved 2014-05-09. **2.** Reeves, Keir; Frost, Lionel; Fahey, Charles (2010). "Integrating the Historiography of the Nineteenth-Century Gold Rushes". *Australian Economic History Review* **50** (2): 111. 3. (<u>ICANN, 2000</u>). **4. & 5.** Article 15 & 16 of CNDRP and rules
6. Article PRC'S Civil Procedure **7.** New Rules for Resolving Chinese Domain Name Disputes - A Comparative Analysis Richard WuSchool of LawUniversity of Hong Kong **8.** New Rules for Resolving Chinese Domain Name Disputes - A Comparative Analysis Richard WuSchool of LawUniversity of Hong Kong **9.** Rule 2(2) CDNDRP and rules **10.** CDNDRP and rules **11.** "Contracting Parties to the Paris Convention". WIPO. Retrieved 2012-12-30.

12. http://www.wipo.int/treaties/en/text.jsp?file_id=288514 Paris Conventionfor the Protection of Industrial Property of March 20, 1883,as revised at Brussels on December 14, 1900,at Washington on June 2, 1911,at The Hague on November 6, 1925,at London on June 2, 1934,at Lisbon on October 31, 1958,and at Stockholm on July 14, 1967,and as amended on September 28, 1979 **13.** See id. **14.** Alternative Dispute Resolution, An Essential Competency for Lawyers, by Mark V.B. Partridge **Oxford University Press (2009). 15.** http://www.ccpit-patent.com.cn/references/Law_Against_Unfair_Competition_China.htm law Against Unfair Competition of The People's Republic of China (Adopted at the Third Session of the Standing Committee of the Eighth National People's Congress on September 2, 1993. Promulgated by Order No. 10 of the President of the People's Republic of China on September 2, 1993. and Effective as of December 1, General Principles of THE Civil Law of the People's Republic of China (Adopted on April 12, 1986) **16, 17, & 18.** Alternative Dispute Resolution, An Essential Competency for Lawyers, by Mark V.B. Partridge **Oxford University Press (2009).**

name Modonna and the domain name Modonna.com. The respondent did not dispute the similarity, but claimed that a disclaimer was posted on the website to ward away any confusion. The ICANN WIPO Arbitration and Mediation center stated, "the disclaimer may be ignored or

1. "Rushes to Statehood, The Oklahoma Land Runs". Dickinson Research Center. Retrieved 2014-05-09. 2. Reeves, Keir; Frost, Lionel; Fahey, Charles (2010). "Integrating the Historiography of the Nineteenth-Century Gold Rushes". *Australian Economic History Review* 50 (2): 111. 3. (ICANN, 2000). 4. & 5. Article 15 & 16 of CNDRP and rules
6. Article PRC'S Civil Procedure 7. New Rules for Resolving Chinese Domain Name Disputes - A Comparative Analysis Richard WuSchool of LawUniversity of Hong Kong 8. New Rules for Resolving Chinese Domain Name Disputes - A Comparative Analysis Richard WuSchool of LawUniversity of Hong Kong 9. Rule 2(2) CDNDRP and rules 10. CDNDRP and rules 11. "Contracting Parties to the Paris Convention". WIPO. Retrieved 2012-12-30.

12. http://www.wipo.int/treaties/en/text.jsp?file_id=288514 Paris Conventionfor the Protection of Industrial Property of March 20, 1883,as revised at Brussels on December 14, 1900,at Washington on June 2, 1911,at The Hague on November 6, 1925,at London on June 2, 1934,at Lisbon on October 31, 1958,and at Stockholm on July 14, 1967,and as amended on September 28, 1979 13. See id. 14. Alternative Dispute Resolution, An Essential Competency for Lawyers, by Mark V.B. Partridge **Oxford University Press (2009). 15.** http://www.ccpit-patent.com.cn/references/Law_Against_Unfair_Competition_China.htm law Against Unfair Competition of The People's Republic of China (Adopted at the Third Session of the Standing Committee of the Eighth National People's Congress on September 2, 1993. Promulgated by Order No. 10 of the President of the People's Republic of China on September 2, 1993. and Effective as of December 1, General Principles of THE Civil Law of the People's Republic of China (Adopted on April 12, 1986) **16, 17, & 18.** Alternative Dispute Resolution, An Essential Competency for Lawyers, by Mark V.B. Partridge **Oxford University Press (2009).**

misunderstood by Internet users, and does nothing to dispel initial interest confusion that is inevitable" finding no merit in this defense. The domain name was found to be 'confusingly similar' to the trademark.

2.   Registration

1. "Rushes to Statehood, The Oklahoma Land Runs". Dickinson Research Center. Retrieved 2014-05-09. 2. Reeves, Keir; Frost, Lionel; Fahey, Charles (2010). "Integrating the Historiography of the Nineteenth-Century Gold Rushes". *Australian Economic History Review* 50 (2): 111. 3. (ICANN, 2000). 4. & 5. Article 15 & 16 of CNDRP and rules
6. Article PRC'S Civil Procedure 7. New Rules for Resolving Chinese Domain Name Disputes - A Comparative Analysis Richard WuSchool of LawUniversity of Hong Kong 8. New Rules for Resolving Chinese Domain Name Disputes - A Comparative Analysis Richard WuSchool of LawUniversity of Hong Kong 9. Rule 2(2) CDNDRP and rules 10. CDNDRP and rules 11. "Contracting Parties to the Paris Convention". WIPO. Retrieved 2012-12-30.

12. http://www.wipo.int/treaties/en/text.jsp?file_id=288514 Paris Conventionfor the Protection of Industrial Property of March 20, 1883,as revised at Brussels on December 14, 1900,at Washington on June 2, 1911,at The Hague on November 6, 1925,at London on June 2, 1934,at Lisbon on October 31, 1958,and at Stockholm on July 14, 1967,and as amended on September 28, 1979 13. See id. 14. Alternative Dispute Resolution, An Essential Competency for Lawyers, by Mark V.B. Partridge **Oxford University Press (2009).** 15. http://www.ccpit-patent.com.cn/references/Law_Against_Unfair_Competition_China.htm law Against Unfair Competition of The People's Republic of China (Adopted at the Third Session of the Standing Committee of the Eighth National People's Congress on September 2, 1993. Promulgated by Order No. 10 of the President of the People's Republic of China on September 2, 1993. and Effective as of December 1, General Principles of THE Civil Law of the People's Republic of China (Adopted on April 12, 1986) **16, 17, & 18.** Alternative Dispute Resolution, An Essential Competency for Lawyers, by Mark V.B. Partridge **Oxford University Press (2009).**

The domain name or trademark must have been registered, and the order of filing is important. Simply checking ICANN'S or CNNIC's database can prove whether a domain name has been registered. Likewise, registration of a trademark can be found where it was

1. "Rushes to Statehood, The Oklahoma Land Runs". Dickinson Research Center. Retrieved 2014-05-09. 2. Reeves, Keir; Frost, Lionel; Fahey, Charles (2010). "Integrating the Historiography of the Nineteenth-Century Gold Rushes". *Australian Economic History Review* 50 (2): 111. 3. (ICANN, 2000). 4. & 5. Article 15 & 16 of CNDRP and rules
6. Article PRC'S Civil Procedure 7. New Rules for Resolving Chinese Domain Name Disputes - A Comparative Analysis Richard WuSchool of LawUniversity of Hong Kong 8. New Rules for Resolving Chinese Domain Name Disputes - A Comparative Analysis Richard WuSchool of LawUniversity of Hong Kong 9. Rule 2(2) CDNDRP and rules 10. CDNDRP and rules 11. "Contracting Parties to the Paris Convention". WIPO. Retrieved 2012-12-30.

12. http://www.wipo.int/treaties/en/text.jsp?file_id=288514 Paris Conventionfor the Protection of Industrial Property of March 20, 1883,as revised at Brussels on December 14, 1900,at Washington on June 2, 1911,at The Hague on November 6, 1925,at London on June 2, 1934,at Lisbon on October 31, 1958,and at Stockholm on July 14, 1967,and as amended on September 28, 1979 13. See id. 14. Alternative Dispute Resolution, An Essential Competency for Lawyers, by Mark V.B. Partridge **Oxford University Press (2009). 15.** http://www.ccpit-patent.com.cn/references/Law_Against_Unfair_Competition_China.htm law Against Unfair Competition of The People's Republic of China (Adopted at the Third Session of the Standing Committee of the Eighth National People's Congress on September 2, 1993. Promulgated by Order No. 10 of the President of the People's Republic of China on September 2, 1993. and Effective as of December 1, General Principles of THE Civil Law of the People's Republic of China (Adopted on April 12, 1986) **16, 17, & 18.** Alternative Dispute Resolution, An Essential Competency for Lawyers, by Mark V.B. Partridge **Oxford University Press (2009).**

registered. Article 4 of the Paris Convention for the Protection of Industrial Property, known as the priority right, states in part: " [A]n applicant from one contracting state shall be able to use its first filing date as the effective filing date in another contracting state, provided the applicant files subsequent

1. "Rushes to Statehood, The Oklahoma Land Runs". Dickinson Research Center. Retrieved 2014-05-09. 2. Reeves, Keir; Frost, Lionel; Fahey, Charles (2010). "Integrating the Historiography of the Nineteenth-Century Gold Rushes". *Australian Economic History Review* **50** (2): 111. 3. (ICANN, 2000). 4. & 5. Article 15 & 16 of CNDRP and rules
6. Article PRC'S Civil Procedure 7. New Rules for Resolving Chinese Domain Name Disputes - A Comparative Analysis Richard WuSchool of LawUniversity of Hong Kong 8. New Rules for Resolving Chinese Domain Name Disputes - A Comparative Analysis Richard WuSchool of LawUniversity of Hong Kong 9. Rule 2(2) CDNDRP and rules 10. CDNDRP and rules 11. "Contracting Parties to the Paris Convention". WIPO. Retrieved 2012-12-30.

12. http://www.wipo.int/treaties/en/text.jsp?file_id=288514 Paris Conventionfor the Protection of Industrial Property of March 20, 1883,as revised at Brussels on December 14, 1900,at Washington on June 2, 1911,at The Hague on November 6, 1925,at London on June 2, 1934,at Lisbon on October 31, 1958,and at Stockholm on July 14, 1967,and as amended on September 28, 1979 13. See id. 14. Alternative Dispute Resolution, An Essential Competency for Lawyers, by Mark V.B. Partridge **Oxford University Press (2009). 15.** http://www.ccpit-patent.com.cn/references/Law_Against_Unfair_Competition_China.htm law Against Unfair Competition of The People's Republic of China (Adopted at the Third Session of the Standing Committee of the Eighth National People's Congress on September 2, 1993. Promulgated by Order No. 10 of the President of the People's Republic of China on September 2, 1993. and Effective as of December 1, General Principles of THE Civil Law of the People's Republic of China (Adopted on April 12, 1986) **16, 17, & 18.** Alternative Dispute Resolution, An Essential Competency for Lawyers, by Mark V.B. Partridge **Oxford University Press (2009).**

applications within 6 months for trademarks, and 12 months for patents" (13). When a client registers a Trademark, either internationally or nationally, they may use that date as the 'first filing' date within any state party to the Paris Convention, which includes 175 countries as of 2013 including China. (14).

1. "Rushes to Statehood, The Oklahoma Land Runs". Dickinson Research Center. Retrieved 2014-05-09. **2.** Reeves, Keir; Frost, Lionel; Fahey, Charles (2010). "Integrating the Historiography of the Nineteenth-Century Gold Rushes". *Australian Economic History Review* **50** (2): 111. 3. (ICANN, 2000). **4. & 5.** Article 15 & 16 of CNDRP and rules
6. Article PRC'S Civil Procedure **7.** New Rules for Resolving Chinese Domain Name Disputes - A Comparative Analysis Richard WuSchool of LawUniversity of Hong Kong **8.** New Rules for Resolving Chinese Domain Name Disputes - A Comparative Analysis Richard WuSchool of LawUniversity of Hong Kong **9.** Rule 2(2) CDNDRP and rules **10.** CDNDRP and rules **11.** "Contracting Parties to the Paris Convention". WIPO. Retrieved 2012-12-30.

12. http://www.wipo.int/treaties/en/text.jsp?file_id=288514 Paris Conventionfor the Protection of Industrial Property of March 20, 1883,as revised at Brussels on December 14, 1900,at Washington on June 2, 1911,at The Hague on November 6, 1925,at London on June 2, 1934,at Lisbon on October 31, 1958,and at Stockholm on July 14, 1967,and as amended on September 28, 1979 **13.** See id. **14.** Alternative Dispute Resolution, An Essential Competency for Lawyers, by Mark V.B. Partridge **Oxford University Press (2009). 15.** http://www.ccpit-patent.com.cn/references/Law_Against_Unfair_Competition_China.htm law Against Unfair Competition of The People's Republic of China (Adopted at the Third Session of the Standing Committee of the Eighth National People's Congress on September 2, 1993. Promulgated by Order No. 10 of the President of the People's Republic of China on September 2, 1993. and Effective as of December 1, General Principles of THE Civil Law of the People's Republic of China (Adopted on April 12, 1986) **16, 17, & 18.** Alternative Dispute Resolution, An Essential Competency for Lawyers, by Mark V.B. Partridge **Oxford University Press (2009).**

In <u>Procter & Gamble Company v. Beijing Guowang Information Co., Ltd.</u>, the trademark 'IKEA' was registered in China with the Trademark Office at the State Administration for Commerce in 1983, and outside China, in 90 different nations. The respondent registered with the

1. "Rushes to Statehood, The Oklahoma Land Runs". Dickinson Research Center. Retrieved 2014-05-09. **2.** Reeves, Keir; Frost, Lionel; Fahey, Charles (2010). "Integrating the Historiography of the Nineteenth-Century Gold Rushes". *Australian Economic History Review* **50** (2): 111. 3. (<u>ICANN, 2000</u>). **4. & 5.** Article 15 & 16 of CNDRP and rules
6. Article PRC'S Civil Procedure **7.** New Rules for Resolving Chinese Domain Name Disputes - A Comparative Analysis Richard WuSchool of LawUniversity of Hong Kong **8**. New Rules for Resolving Chinese Domain Name Disputes - A Comparative Analysis Richard WuSchool of LawUniversity of Hong Kong **9.** Rule 2(2) CDNDRP and rules **10.** CDNDRP and rules **11.** "Contracting Parties to the Paris Convention". WIPO. Retrieved 2012-12-30.

12. http://www.wipo.int/treaties/en/text.jsp?file_id=288514 Paris Conventionfor the Protection of Industrial Property of March 20, 1883,as revised at Brussels on December 14, 1900,at Washington on June 2, 1911,at The Hague on November 6, 1925,at London on June 2, 1934,at Lisbon on October 31, 1958,and at Stockholm on July 14, 1967,and as amended on September 28, 1979 **13.** See id. **14.** Alternative Dispute Resolution, An Essential Competency for Lawyers, by Mark V.B. Partridge **Oxford University Press (2009). 15.** http://www.ccpit-patent.com.cn/references/Law_Against_Unfair_Competition_China.htm law Against Unfair Competition of The People's Republic of China (Adopted at the Third Session of the Standing Committee of the Eighth National People's Congress on September 2, 1993. Promulgated by Order No. 10 of the President of the People's Republic of China on September 2, 1993. and Effective as of December 1, General Principles of THE Civil Law of the People's Republic of China (Adopted on April 12, 1986) **16, 17, & 18.** Alternative Dispute Resolution, An Essential Competency for Lawyers, by Mark V.B. Partridge **Oxford University Press (2009).**

CNNIC in 1997, and the CNDRC found for the complainant.

However in <u>Mercer Human Resource Consulting, Inc. v. Meyth International Consulting Co., Ltd.</u>, the trademark 'Mercer' was registered outside of China, but had not completed registration of the

1. "Rushes to Statehood, The Oklahoma Land Runs". Dickinson Research Center. Retrieved 2014-05-09. **2.** Reeves, Keir; Frost, Lionel; Fahey, Charles (2010). "Integrating the Historiography of the Nineteenth-Century Gold Rushes". *Australian Economic History Review* **50** (2): 111. 3. (<u>ICANN, 2000</u>). **4. & 5.** Article 15 & 16 of CNDRP and rules
6. Article PRC'S Civil Procedure **7.** New Rules for Resolving Chinese Domain Name Disputes - A Comparative Analysis Richard WuSchool of LawUniversity of Hong Kong **8.** New Rules for Resolving Chinese Domain Name Disputes - A Comparative Analysis Richard WuSchool of LawUniversity of Hong Kong **9.** Rule 2(2) CDNDRP and rules **10.** CDNDRP and rules **11.** "Contracting Parties to the Paris Convention". WIPO. Retrieved 2012-12-30.

12. http://www.wipo.int/treaties/en/text.jsp?file_id=288514 Paris Conventionfor the Protection of Industrial Property of March 20, 1883,as revised at Brussels on December 14, 1900,at Washington on June 2, 1911,at The Hague on November 6, 1925,at London on June 2, 1934,at Lisbon on October 31, 1958,and at Stockholm on July 14, 1967,and as amended on September 28, 1979 **13.** See id. **14.** Alternative Dispute Resolution, An Essential Competency for Lawyers, by Mark V.B. Partridge **Oxford University Press (2009). 15.** http://www.ccpit-patent.com.cn/references/Law_Against_Unfair_Competition_China.htm law Against Unfair Competition of The People's Republic of China (Adopted at the Third Session of the Standing Committee of the Eighth National People's Congress on September 2, 1993. Promulgated by Order No. 10 of the President of the People's Republic of China on September 2, 1993. and Effective as of December 1, General Principles of THE Civil Law of the People's Republic of China (Adopted on April 12, 1986) **16, 17, & 18.** Alternative Dispute Resolution, An Essential Competency for Lawyers, by Mark V.B. Partridge **Oxford University Press (2009).**

trademark within China. The CDNDRC, Beijing High People's Court, and Supreme People's Court found in favor of the Complainant that under Article 2 of the Paris Convention even though the complainant has not completed registration because it has establish a close relationship

1. "Rushes to Statehood, The Oklahoma Land Runs". Dickinson Research Center. Retrieved 2014-05-09. 2. Reeves, Keir; Frost, Lionel; Fahey, Charles (2010). "Integrating the Historiography of the Nineteenth-Century Gold Rushes". *Australian Economic History Review* 50 (2): 111. 3. (ICANN, 2000). 4. & 5. Article 15 & 16 of CNDRP and rules
6. Article PRC'S Civil Procedure 7. New Rules for Resolving Chinese Domain Name Disputes - A Comparative Analysis Richard WuSchool of LawUniversity of Hong Kong 8. New Rules for Resolving Chinese Domain Name Disputes - A Comparative Analysis Richard WuSchool of LawUniversity of Hong Kong 9. Rule 2(2) CDNDRP and rules 10. CDNDRP and rules 11. "Contracting Parties to the Paris Convention". WIPO. Retrieved 2012-12-30.

12. http://www.wipo.int/treaties/en/text.jsp?file_id=288514 Paris Conventionfor the Protection of Industrial Property of March 20, 1883,as revised at Brussels on December 14, 1900,at Washington on June 2, 1911,at The Hague on November 6, 1925,at London on June 2, 1934,at Lisbon on October 31, 1958,and at Stockholm on July 14, 1967,and as amended on September 28, 1979 13. See id. 14. Alternative Dispute Resolution, An Essential Competency for Lawyers, by Mark V.B. Partridge Oxford University Press (2009). 15. http://www.ccpit-patent.com.cn/references/Law_Against_Unfair_Competition_China.htm law Against Unfair Competition of The People's Republic of China (Adopted at the Third Session of the Standing Committee of the Eighth National People's Congress on September 2, 1993. Promulgated by Order No. 10 of the President of the People's Republic of China on September 2, 1993. and Effective as of December 1, General Principles of THE Civil Law of the People's Republic of China (Adopted on April 12, 1986) 16, 17, & 18. Alternative Dispute Resolution, An Essential Competency for Lawyers, by Mark V.B. Partridge Oxford University Press (2009).

between it in China and the rest of the world.

And in <u>Procter & Gamble Company v. Shnhai Chenxuan Technology and Trade Co. Ltd</u>, the trademark 'SafeGuard' was registered as apart of the packaging and advertisements all before 2000. The respondent registered the domain name in

1. "Rushes to Statehood, The Oklahoma Land Runs". Dickinson Research Center. Retrieved 2014-05-09. 2. Reeves, Keir; Frost, Lionel; Fahey, Charles (2010). "Integrating the Historiography of the Nineteenth-Century Gold Rushes". *Australian Economic History Review* 50 (2): 111. 3. (ICANN, 2000). 4. & 5. Article 15 & 16 of CNDRP and rules
6. Article PRC'S Civil Procedure 7. New Rules for Resolving Chinese Domain Name Disputes - A Comparative Analysis Richard WuSchool of LawUniversity of Hong Kong 8. New Rules for Resolving Chinese Domain Name Disputes - A Comparative Analysis Richard WuSchool of LawUniversity of Hong Kong 9. Rule 2(2) CDNDRP and rules 10. CDNDRP and rules 11. "Contracting Parties to the Paris Convention". WIPO. Retrieved 2012-12-30.

12. http://www.wipo.int/treaties/en/text.jsp?file_id=288514 Paris Conventionfor the Protection of Industrial Property of March 20, 1883,as revised at Brussels on December 14, 1900,at Washington on June 2, 1911,at The Hague on November 6, 1925,at London on June 2, 1934,at Lisbon on October 31, 1958,and at Stockholm on July 14, 1967,and as amended on September 28, 1979 13. See id. 14. Alternative Dispute Resolution, An Essential Competency for Lawyers, by Mark V.B. Partridge **Oxford University Press (2009). 15.** http://www.ccpit-patent.com.cn/references/Law_Against_Unfair_Competition_China.htm law Against Unfair Competition of The People's Republic of China (Adopted at the Third Session of the Standing Committee of the Eighth National People's Congress on September 2, 1993. Promulgated by Order No. 10 of the President of the People's Republic of China on September 2, 1993. and Effective as of December 1, General Principles of THE Civil Law of the People's Republic of China (Adopted on April 12, 1986) **16, 17, & 18.** Alternative Dispute Resolution, An Essential Competency for Lawyers, by Mark V.B. Partridge **Oxford University Press (2009).**

2000 twice, and the CNDRC and PRC found in favor of P&G.

However in <u>Madonna Ciccone, v. Dan Parisi</u>, the trademark was never registered because it was apart of the personality and famous name Modonna. The ICANN'S WIPO Arbitration and

1. "Rushes to Statehood, The Oklahoma Land Runs". Dickinson Research Center. Retrieved 2014-05-09. 2. Reeves, Keir; Frost, Lionel; Fahey, Charles (2010). "Integrating the Historiography of the Nineteenth-Century Gold Rushes". *Australian Economic History Review* **50** (2): 111. 3. (ICANN, 2000). **4. & 5.** Article 15 & 16 of CNDRP and rules

6. Article PRC'S Civil Procedure 7. New Rules for Resolving Chinese Domain Name Disputes - A Comparative Analysis Richard WuSchool of LawUniversity of Hong Kong 8. New Rules for Resolving Chinese Domain Name Disputes - A Comparative Analysis Richard WuSchool of LawUniversity of Hong Kong 9. Rule 2(2) CDNDRP and rules 10. CDNDRP and rules 11. "Contracting Parties to the Paris Convention". WIPO. Retrieved 2012-12-30.

12. http://www.wipo.int/treaties/en/text.jsp?file_id=288514 Paris Conventionfor the Protection of Industrial Property of March 20, 1883,as revised at Brussels on December 14, 1900,at Washington on June 2, 1911,at The Hague on November 6, 1925,at London on June 2, 1934,at Lisbon on October 31, 1958,and at Stockholm on July 14, 1967,and as amended on September 28, 1979 13. See id. 14. Alternative Dispute Resolution, An Essential Competency for Lawyers, by Mark V.B. Partridge **Oxford University Press (2009). 15.** http://www.ccpit-patent.com.cn/references/Law_Against_Unfair_Competition_China.htm law Against Unfair Competition of The People's Republic of China (Adopted at the Third Session of the Standing Committee of the Eighth National People's Congress on September 2, 1993. Promulgated by Order No. 10 of the President of the People's Republic of China on September 2, 1993. and Effective as of December 1, General Principles of THE Civil Law of the People's Republic of China (Adopted on April 12, 1986) **16, 17, & 18.** Alternative Dispute Resolution, An Essential Competency for Lawyers, by Mark V.B. Partridge **Oxford University Press (2009).**

Mediation found in favor of the complainant, even though the respondent has registered the trademark properly stating ' it would be a mistake to conclude that mere registration of a trademark creates a legitimate interest under the Policy. To establish cognizable rights, the overall circumstances should

1. "Rushes to Statehood, The Oklahoma Land Runs". Dickinson Research Center. Retrieved 2014-05-09. **2.** Reeves, Keir; Frost, Lionel; Fahey, Charles (2010). "Integrating the Historiography of the Nineteenth-Century Gold Rushes". *Australian Economic History Review* **50** (2): 111. 3. (ICANN, 2000). **4. & 5.** Article 15 & 16 of CNDRP and rules
6. Article PRC'S Civil Procedure **7.** New Rules for Resolving Chinese Domain Name Disputes - A Comparative Analysis Richard WuSchool of LawUniversity of Hong Kong **8.** New Rules for Resolving Chinese Domain Name Disputes - A Comparative Analysis Richard WuSchool of LawUniversity of Hong Kong **9.** Rule 2(2) CDNDRP and rules **10.** CDNDRP and rules **11.** "Contracting Parties to the Paris Convention". WIPO. Retrieved 2012-12-30.

12. http://www.wipo.int/treaties/en/text.jsp?file_id=288514 Paris Conventionfor the Protection of Industrial Property of March 20, 1883,as revised at Brussels on December 14, 1900,at Washington on June 2, 1911,at The Hague on November 6, 1925,at London on June 2, 1934,at Lisbon on October 31, 1958,and at Stockholm on July 14, 1967,and as amended on September 28, 1979 **13.** See id. **14.** Alternative Dispute Resolution, An Essential Competency for Lawyers, by Mark V.B. Partridge **Oxford University Press (2009). 15.** http://www.ccpit-patent.com.cn/references/Law_Against_Unfair_Competition_China.htm law Against Unfair Competition of The People's Republic of China (Adopted at the Third Session of the Standing Committee of the Eighth National People's Congress on September 2, 1993. Promulgated by Order No. 10 of the President of the People's Republic of China on September 2, 1993. and Effective as of December 1, General Principles of THE Civil Law of the People's Republic of China (Adopted on April 12, 1986) **16, 17, & 18.** Alternative Dispute Resolution, An Essential Competency for Lawyers, by Mark V.B. Partridge **Oxford University Press (2009).**

demonstrate that the registration was obtained in good faith for the purpose of making bona fide use of the mark in the jurisdiction where the mark is registered, and not obtained merely to circumvent the application of the Policy." (14)

1. "Rushes to Statehood, The Oklahoma Land Runs". Dickinson Research Center. Retrieved 2014-05-09. 2. Reeves, Keir; Frost, Lionel; Fahey, Charles (2010). "Integrating the Historiography of the Nineteenth-Century Gold Rushes". *Australian Economic History Review* 50 (2): 111. 3. (ICANN, 2000). 4. & 5. Article 15 & 16 of CNDRP and rules
6. Article PRC'S Civil Procedure 7. New Rules for Resolving Chinese Domain Name Disputes - A Comparative Analysis Richard WuSchool of LawUniversity of Hong Kong 8. New Rules for Resolving Chinese Domain Name Disputes - A Comparative Analysis Richard WuSchool of LawUniversity of Hong Kong 9. Rule 2(2) CDNDRP and rules 10. CDNDRP and rules 11. "Contracting Parties to the Paris Convention". WIPO. Retrieved 2012-12-30.

12. http://www.wipo.int/treaties/en/text.jsp?file_id=288514 Paris Conventionfor the Protection of Industrial Property of March 20, 1883,as revised at Brussels on December 14, 1900,at Washington on June 2, 1911,at The Hague on November 6, 1925,at London on June 2, 1934,at Lisbon on October 31, 1958,and at Stockholm on July 14, 1967,and as amended on September 28, 1979 13. See id. 14. Alternative Dispute Resolution, An Essential Competency for Lawyers, by Mark V.B. Partridge **Oxford University Press (2009).** 15. http://www.ccpit-patent.com.cn/references/Law_Against_Unfair_Competition_China.htm law Against Unfair Competition of The People's Republic of China (Adopted at the Third Session of the Standing Committee of the Eighth National People's Congress on September 2, 1993. Promulgated by Order No. 10 of the President of the People's Republic of China on September 2, 1993. and Effective as of December 1, General Principles of THE Civil Law of the People's Republic of China (Adopted on April 12, 1986) **16, 17, & 18.** Alternative Dispute Resolution, An Essential Competency for Lawyers, by Mark V.B. Partridge **Oxford University Press (2009).**

3.   Bad Faith

Bad faith is registering and using a domain name knowing or failing to know that a trademark owner has established a degree of popularity with consumers and trade practices infringing their IPR's, which may be active or passive. Article 6 of

1. "Rushes to Statehood, The Oklahoma Land Runs". Dickinson Research Center. Retrieved 2014-05-09. 2. Reeves, Keir; Frost, Lionel; Fahey, Charles (2010). "Integrating the Historiography of the Nineteenth-Century Gold Rushes". *Australian Economic History Review* 50 (2): 111. 3. (ICANN, 2000). 4. & 5. Article 15 & 16 of CNDRP and rules
6. Article PRC'S Civil Procedure 7. New Rules for Resolving Chinese Domain Name Disputes - A Comparative Analysis Richard WuSchool of LawUniversity of Hong Kong 8. New Rules for Resolving Chinese Domain Name Disputes - A Comparative Analysis Richard WuSchool of LawUniversity of Hong Kong 9. Rule 2(2) CDNDRP and rules 10. CDNDRP and rules 11. "Contracting Parties to the Paris Convention". WIPO. Retrieved 2012-12-30.

12. http://www.wipo.int/treaties/en/text.jsp?file_id=288514 Paris Conventionfor the Protection of Industrial Property of March 20, 1883,as revised at Brussels on December 14, 1900,at Washington on June 2, 1911,at The Hague on November 6, 1925,at London on June 2, 1934,at Lisbon on October 31, 1958,and at Stockholm on July 14, 1967,and as amended on September 28, 1979 13. See id. 14. Alternative Dispute Resolution, An Essential Competency for Lawyers, by Mark V.B. Partridge **Oxford University Press (2009).** 15. http://www.ccpit-patent.com.cn/references/Law_Against_Unfair_Competition_China.htm law Against Unfair Competition of The People's Republic of China (Adopted at the Third Session of the Standing Committee of the Eighth National People's Congress on September 2, 1993. Promulgated by Order No. 10 of the President of the People's Republic of China on September 2, 1993. and Effective as of December 1, General Principles of THE Civil Law of the People's Republic of China (Adopted on April 12, 1986) **16, 17, & 18.** Alternative Dispute Resolution, An Essential Competency for Lawyers, by Mark V.B. Partridge **Oxford University Press (2009).**

Interpretations of The Supreme People's Court on Several Issues Concerning the Application of Law to the Trial of Cases of Civil Disputes over the Protection of Famous Trademarks stipulates states in parts: " A shop name in the name of enterprise that has certain market popularity and is

1. "Rushes to Statehood, The Oklahoma Land Runs". Dickinson Research Center. Retrieved 2014-05-09. **2.** Reeves, Keir; Frost, Lionel; Fahey, Charles (2010). "Integrating the Historiography of the Nineteenth-Century Gold Rushes". *Australian Economic History Review* **50** (2): 111. 3. (ICANN, 2000). **4. & 5.** Article 15 & 16 of CNDRP and rules
6. Article PRC'S Civil Procedure **7.** New Rules for Resolving Chinese Domain Name Disputes - A Comparative Analysis Richard WuSchool of LawUniversity of Hong Kong **8.** New Rules for Resolving Chinese Domain Name Disputes - A Comparative Analysis Richard WuSchool of LawUniversity of Hong Kong **9.** Rule 2(2) CDNDRP and rules **10.** CDNDRP and rules **11.** "Contracting Parties to the Paris Convention". WIPO. Retrieved 2012-12-30.

12. http://www.wipo.int/treaties/en/text.jsp?file_id=288514 Paris Conventionfor the Protection of Industrial Property of March 20, 1883,as revised at Brussels on December 14, 1900,at Washington on June 2, 1911,at The Hague on November 6, 1925,at London on June 2, 1934,at Lisbon on October 31, 1958,and at Stockholm on July 14, 1967,and as amended on September 28, 1979 **13.** See id. **14.** Alternative Dispute Resolution, An Essential Competency for Lawyers, by Mark V.B. Partridge **Oxford University Press (2009). 15.** http://www.ccpit-patent.com.cn/references/Law_Against_Unfair_Competition_China.htm law Against Unfair Competition of The People's Republic of China (Adopted at the Third Session of the Standing Committee of the Eighth National People's Congress on September 2, 1993. Promulgated by Order No. 10 of the President of the People's Republic of China on September 2, 1993. and Effective as of December 1, General Principles of THE Civil Law of the People's Republic of China (Adopted on April 12, 1986) **16, 17, & 18.** Alternative Dispute Resolution, An Essential Competency for Lawyers, by Mark V.B. Partridge **Oxford University Press (2009).**

acknowledged by the public concerned may be ascertained as an enterprise name as stipulated in Subparagraph (c) of Article 5 of The Anti-unfair Competition Law."

And Under PRC's civil law, a client enjoys the PRC's Law Against Unfair Competition Conduct and the General

1. "Rushes to Statehood, The Oklahoma Land Runs". Dickinson Research Center. Retrieved 2014-05-09. 2. Reeves, Keir; Frost, Lionel; Fahey, Charles (2010). "Integrating the Historiography of the Nineteenth-Century Gold Rushes". *Australian Economic History Review* 50 (2): 111. 3. (ICANN, 2000). 4. & 5. Article 15 & 16 of CNDRP and rules
6. Article PRC'S Civil Procedure 7. New Rules for Resolving Chinese Domain Name Disputes - A Comparative Analysis Richard WuSchool of LawUniversity of Hong Kong 8. New Rules for Resolving Chinese Domain Name Disputes - A Comparative Analysis Richard WuSchool of LawUniversity of Hong Kong 9. Rule 2(2) CDNDRP and rules 10. CDNDRP and rules 11. "Contracting Parties to the Paris Convention". WIPO. Retrieved 2012-12-30.

12. http://www.wipo.int/treaties/en/text.jsp?file_id=288514 Paris Conventionfor the Protection of Industrial Property of March 20, 1883,as revised at Brussels on December 14, 1900,at Washington on June 2, 1911,at The Hague on November 6, 1925,at London on June 2, 1934,at Lisbon on October 31, 1958,and at Stockholm on July 14, 1967,and as amended on September 28, 1979 13. See id. 14. Alternative Dispute Resolution, An Essential Competency for Lawyers, by Mark V.B. Partridge **Oxford University Press (2009). 15.** http://www.ccpit-patent.com.cn/references/Law_Against_Unfair_Competition_China.htm law Against Unfair Competition of The People's Republic of China (Adopted at the Third Session of the Standing Committee of the Eighth National People's Congress on September 2, 1993. Promulgated by Order No. 10 of the President of the People's Republic of China on September 2, 1993. and Effective as of December 1, General Principles of THE Civil Law of the People's Republic of China (Adopted on April 12, 1986) **16, 17, & 18.** Alternative Dispute Resolution, An Essential Competency for Lawyers, by Mark V.B. Partridge **Oxford University Press (2009).**

Principles of the Civil Law of the PRC. The Law Against Unfair Competition of the PRC states in parts: "An operator shall, in transactions in the market, follow the he principle of voluntariness, equality, fairness, honesty and credibility, and observe generally recognized business

1. "Rushes to Statehood, The Oklahoma Land Runs". Dickinson Research Center. Retrieved 2014-05-09. 2. Reeves, Keir; Frost, Lionel; Fahey, Charles (2010). "Integrating the Historiography of the Nineteenth-Century Gold Rushes". *Australian Economic History Review* 50 (2): 111. 3. (ICANN, 2000). 4. & 5. Article 15 & 16 of CNDRP and rules
6. Article PRC'S Civil Procedure 7. New Rules for Resolving Chinese Domain Name Disputes - A Comparative Analysis Richard WuSchool of LawUniversity of Hong Kong 8. New Rules for Resolving Chinese Domain Name Disputes - A Comparative Analysis Richard WuSchool of LawUniversity of Hong Kong 9. Rule 2(2) CDNDRP and rules 10. CDNDRP and rules 11. "Contracting Parties to the Paris Convention". WIPO. Retrieved 2012-12-30.

12. http://www.wipo.int/treaties/en/text.jsp?file_id=288514 Paris Conventionfor the Protection of Industrial Property of March 20, 1883,as revised at Brussels on December 14, 1900,at Washington on June 2, 1911,at The Hague on November 6, 1925,at London on June 2, 1934,at Lisbon on October 31, 1958,and at Stockholm on July 14, 1967,and as amended on September 28, 1979 13. See id. 14. Alternative Dispute Resolution, An Essential Competency for Lawyers, by Mark V.B. Partridge **Oxford University Press (2009). 15.** http://www.ccpit-patent.com.cn/references/Law_Against_Unfair_Competition_China.htm law Against Unfair Competition of The People's Republic of China (Adopted at the Third Session of the Standing Committee of the Eighth National People's Congress on September 2, 1993. Promulgated by Order No. 10 of the President of the People's Republic of China on September 2, 1993. and Effective as of December 1, General Principles of THE Civil Law of the People's Republic of China (Adopted on April 12, 1986) **16, 17, & 18.** Alternative Dispute Resolution, An Essential Competency for Lawyers, by Mark V.B. Partridge **Oxford University Press (2009).**

ethics. "Unfair competition" in this Law refers to acts of operator, which contravene the provisions of this Law, damage the lawful rights and interests of other operator, and disturb the socio-economic order" (15). And, the General Principles of the Civil Law of the PRC states in parts: "In civil activities, the

1. "Rushes to Statehood, The Oklahoma Land Runs". Dickinson Research Center. Retrieved 2014-05-09. 2. Reeves, Keir; Frost, Lionel; Fahey, Charles (2010). "Integrating the Historiography of the Nineteenth-Century Gold Rushes". *Australian Economic History Review* 50 (2): 111. 3. (ICANN, 2000). 4. & 5. Article 15 & 16 of CNDRP and rules
6. Article PRC'S Civil Procedure 7. New Rules for Resolving Chinese Domain Name Disputes - A Comparative Analysis Richard WuSchool of LawUniversity of Hong Kong 8. New Rules for Resolving Chinese Domain Name Disputes - A Comparative Analysis Richard WuSchool of LawUniversity of Hong Kong 9. Rule 2(2) CDNDRP and rules 10. CDNDRP and rules 11. "Contracting Parties to the Paris Convention". WIPO. Retrieved 2012-12-30.

12. http://www.wipo.int/treaties/en/text.jsp?file_id=288514 Paris Conventionfor the Protection of Industrial Property of March 20, 1883,as revised at Brussels on December 14, 1900,at Washington on June 2, 1911,at The Hague on November 6, 1925,at London on June 2, 1934,at Lisbon on October 31, 1958,and at Stockholm on July 14, 1967,and as amended on September 28, 1979 13. See id. 14. Alternative Dispute Resolution, An Essential Competency for Lawyers, by Mark V.B. Partridge **Oxford University Press (2009).** 15. http://www.ccpit-patent.com.cn/references/Law_Against_Unfair_Competition_China.htm law Against Unfair Competition of The People's Republic of China (Adopted at the Third Session of the Standing Committee of the Eighth National People's Congress on September 2, 1993. Promulgated by Order No. 10 of the President of the People's Republic of China on September 2, 1993. and Effective as of December 1, General Principles of THE Civil Law of the People's Republic of China (Adopted on April 12, 1986) **16, 17, & 18.** Alternative Dispute Resolution, An Essential Competency for Lawyers, by Mark V.B. Partridge **Oxford University Press (2009).**

principles of voluntariness, fairness, making compensation for equal value, honesty and credibility shall be observed" (16). When a client establishing that their trademark is 'well-known', the domain holder will have registered under bad faith, however, additional evidence is required to prove bad faith use.

1. "Rushes to Statehood, The Oklahoma Land Runs". Dickinson Research Center. Retrieved 2014-05-09. 2. Reeves, Keir; Frost, Lionel; Fahey, Charles (2010). "Integrating the Historiography of the Nineteenth-Century Gold Rushes". *Australian Economic History Review* 50 (2): 111. 3. (ICANN, 2000). 4. & 5. Article 15 & 16 of CNDRP and rules
6. Article PRC'S Civil Procedure 7. New Rules for Resolving Chinese Domain Name Disputes - A Comparative Analysis Richard WuSchool of LawUniversity of Hong Kong 8. New Rules for Resolving Chinese Domain Name Disputes - A Comparative Analysis Richard WuSchool of LawUniversity of Hong Kong 9. Rule 2(2) CDNDRP and rules 10. CDNDRP and rules 11. "Contracting Parties to the Paris Convention". WIPO. Retrieved 2012-12-30.

12. http://www.wipo.int/treaties/en/text.jsp?file_id=288514 Paris Conventionfor the Protection of Industrial Property of March 20, 1883,as revised at Brussels on December 14, 1900,at Washington on June 2, 1911,at The Hague on November 6, 1925,at London on June 2, 1934,at Lisbon on October 31, 1958,and at Stockholm on July 14, 1967,and as amended on September 28, 1979 13. See id. 14. Alternative Dispute Resolution, An Essential Competency for Lawyers, by Mark V.B. Partridge **Oxford University Press (2009). 15.** http://www.ccpit-patent.com.cn/references/Law_Against_Unfair_Competition_China.htm law Against Unfair Competition of The People's Republic of China (Adopted at the Third Session of the Standing Committee of the Eighth National People's Congress on September 2, 1993. Promulgated by Order No. 10 of the President of the People's Republic of China on September 2, 1993. and Effective as of December 1, General Principles of THE Civil Law of the People's Republic of China (Adopted on April 12, 1986) **16, 17, & 18.** Alternative Dispute Resolution, An Essential Competency for Lawyers, by Mark V.B. Partridge **Oxford University Press (2009).**

In <u>Procter & Gamble Company v. Beijing Guowang Information Co., Ltd.</u>, the trademark 'IKEA' has been used since 1998 in Shanghai and Beijing, and P&G has spent over 6 million RMB in advertising and promotion, which increased to 17 million RMB in 1999. The respondent

1. "Rushes to Statehood, The Oklahoma Land Runs". Dickinson Research Center. Retrieved 2014-05-09. 2. Reeves, Keir; Frost, Lionel; Fahey, Charles (2010). "Integrating the Historiography of the Nineteenth-Century Gold Rushes". *Australian Economic History Review* **50** (2): 111. 3. (ICANN, 2000). 4. & 5. Article 15 & 16 of CNDRP and rules
6. Article PRC'S Civil Procedure 7. New Rules for Resolving Chinese Domain Name Disputes - A Comparative Analysis Richard WuSchool of LawUniversity of Hong Kong 8. New Rules for Resolving Chinese Domain Name Disputes - A Comparative Analysis Richard WuSchool of LawUniversity of Hong Kong 9. Rule 2(2) CDNDRP and rules 10. CDNDRP and rules 11. "Contracting Parties to the Paris Convention". WIPO. Retrieved 2012-12-30.

12. http://www.wipo.int/treaties/en/text.jsp?file_id=288514 Paris Conventionfor the Protection of Industrial Property of March 20, 1883,as revised at Brussels on December 14, 1900,at Washington on June 2, 1911,at The Hague on November 6, 1925,at London on June 2, 1934,at Lisbon on October 31, 1958,and at Stockholm on July 14, 1967,and as amended on September 28, 1979 13. See id. 14. Alternative Dispute Resolution, An Essential Competency for Lawyers, by Mark V.B. Partridge **Oxford University Press (2009).** 15. http://www.ccpit-patent.com.cn/references/Law_Against_Unfair_Competition_China.htm law Against Unfair Competition of The People's Republic of China (Adopted at the Third Session of the Standing Committee of the Eighth National People's Congress on September 2, 1993. Promulgated by Order No. 10 of the President of the People's Republic of China on September 2, 1993. and Effective as of December 1, General Principles of THE Civil Law of the People's Republic of China (Adopted on April 12, 1986) **16, 17, & 18.** Alternative Dispute Resolution, An Essential Competency for Lawyers, by Mark V.B. Partridge **Oxford University Press (2009).**

had registered multiple domain names associated with 'well-known' trademarks, and left them unused for long periods of time. The PRC's civil court found that even when speculating the respondent's intentions, the fact it was unable to provide evidence that the site was being used for a

1. "Rushes to Statehood, The Oklahoma Land Runs". Dickinson Research Center. Retrieved 2014-05-09. **2.** Reeves, Keir; Frost, Lionel; Fahey, Charles (2010). "Integrating the Historiography of the Nineteenth-Century Gold Rushes". *Australian Economic History Review* **50** (2): 111. 3. (ICANN, 2000). **4. & 5.** Article 15 & 16 of CNDRP and rules
6. Article PRC'S Civil Procedure **7.** New Rules for Resolving Chinese Domain Name Disputes - A Comparative Analysis Richard WuSchool of LawUniversity of Hong Kong **8.** New Rules for Resolving Chinese Domain Name Disputes - A Comparative Analysis Richard WuSchool of LawUniversity of Hong Kong **9.** Rule 2(2) CDNDRP and rules **10.** CDNDRP and rules **11.** "Contracting Parties to the Paris Convention". WIPO. Retrieved 2012-12-30.

12. http://www.wipo.int/treaties/en/text.jsp?file_id=288514 Paris Conventionfor the Protection of Industrial Property of March 20, 1883,as revised at Brussels on December 14, 1900,at Washington on June 2, 1911,at The Hague on November 6, 1925,at London on June 2, 1934,at Lisbon on October 31, 1958,and at Stockholm on July 14, 1967,and as amended on September 28, 1979 **13.** See id. **14.** Alternative Dispute Resolution, An Essential Competency for Lawyers, by Mark V.B. Partridge **Oxford University Press (2009).** **15.** http://www.ccpit-patent.com.cn/references/Law_Against_Unfair_Competition_China.htm law Against Unfair Competition of The People's Republic of China (Adopted at the Third Session of the Standing Committee of the Eighth National People's Congress on September 2, 1993. Promulgated by Order No. 10 of the President of the People's Republic of China on September 2, 1993. and Effective as of December 1, General Principles of THE Civil Law of the People's Republic of China (Adopted on April 12, 1986) **16, 17, & 18.** Alternative Dispute Resolution, An Essential Competency for Lawyers, by Mark V.B. Partridge **Oxford University Press (2009).**

bona fide good faith reason for services or goods, it had registered and used the site in bad faith. The domain name was transferred to the complainant.

However in <u>Mercer Human Resource Consulting, Inc. v. Meyth International Consulting Co., Ltd.</u>, the complainant

1. "Rushes to Statehood, The Oklahoma Land Runs". Dickinson Research Center. Retrieved 2014-05-09. 2. Reeves, Keir; Frost, Lionel; Fahey, Charles (2010). "Integrating the Historiography of the Nineteenth-Century Gold Rushes". *Australian Economic History Review* 50 (2): 111. 3. (ICANN, 2000). 4. & 5. Article 15 & 16 of CNDRP and rules
6. Article PRC'S Civil Procedure 7. New Rules for Resolving Chinese Domain Name Disputes - A Comparative Analysis Richard WuSchool of LawUniversity of Hong Kong 8. New Rules for Resolving Chinese Domain Name Disputes - A Comparative Analysis Richard WuSchool of LawUniversity of Hong Kong 9. Rule 2(2) CDNDRP and rules 10. CDNDRP and rules 11. "Contracting Parties to the Paris Convention". WIPO. Retrieved 2012-12-30.

12. http://www.wipo.int/treaties/en/text.jsp?file_id=288514 Paris Conventionfor the Protection of Industrial Property of March 20, 1883,as revised at Brussels on December 14, 1900,at Washington on June 2, 1911,at The Hague on November 6, 1925,at London on June 2, 1934,at Lisbon on October 31, 1958,and at Stockholm on July 14, 1967,and as amended on September 28, 1979 13. See id. 14. Alternative Dispute Resolution, An Essential Competency for Lawyers, by Mark V.B. Partridge Oxford University Press (2009). 15. http://www.ccpit-patent.com.cn/references/Law_Against_Unfair_Competition_China.htm law Against Unfair Competition of The People's Republic of China (Adopted at the Third Session of the Standing Committee of the Eighth National People's Congress on September 2, 1993. Promulgated by Order No. 10 of the President of the People's Republic of China on September 2, 1993. and Effective as of December 1, General Principles of THE Civil Law of the People's Republic of China (Adopted on April 12, 1986) 16, 17, & 18. Alternative Dispute Resolution, An Essential Competency for Lawyers, by Mark V.B. Partridge Oxford University Press (2009).

argued there was no business connection between them and the respondent, they were part of the same industry, that it has established a close relationship between China and the rest of the world, and the trademark had nothing to do with the respondents business. After appealing to Beijing Court, the

1. "Rushes to Statehood, The Oklahoma Land Runs". Dickinson Research Center. Retrieved 2014-05-09. 2. Reeves, Keir; Frost, Lionel; Fahey, Charles (2010). "Integrating the Historiography of the Nineteenth-Century Gold Rushes". *Australian Economic History Review* 50 (2): 111. 3. (ICANN, 2000). 4. & 5. Article 15 & 16 of CNDRP and rules

6. Article PRC'S Civil Procedure 7. New Rules for Resolving Chinese Domain Name Disputes - A Comparative Analysis Richard WuSchool of LawUniversity of Hong Kong 8. New Rules for Resolving Chinese Domain Name Disputes - A Comparative Analysis Richard WuSchool of LawUniversity of Hong Kong 9. Rule 2(2) CDNDRP and rules 10. CDNDRP and rules 11. "Contracting Parties to the Paris Convention". WIPO. Retrieved 2012-12-30.

12. http://www.wipo.int/treaties/en/text.jsp?file_id=288514 Paris Conventionfor the Protection of Industrial Property of March 20, 1883,as revised at Brussels on December 14, 1900,at Washington on June 2, 1911,at The Hague on November 6, 1925,at London on June 2, 1934,at Lisbon on October 31, 1958,and at Stockholm on July 14, 1967,and as amended on September 28, 1979 13. See id. 14. Alternative Dispute Resolution, An Essential Competency for Lawyers, by Mark V.B. Partridge **Oxford University Press (2009).** 15. http://www.ccpit-patent.com.cn/references/Law_Against_Unfair_Competition_China.htm law Against Unfair Competition of The People's Republic of China (Adopted at the Third Session of the Standing Committee of the Eighth National People's Congress on September 2, 1993. Promulgated by Order No. 10 of the President of the People's Republic of China on September 2, 1993. and Effective as of December 1, General Principles of THE Civil Law of the People's Republic of China (Adopted on April 12, 1986) **16, 17, & 18.** Alternative Dispute Resolution, An Essential Competency for Lawyers, by Mark V.B. Partridge **Oxford University Press (2009).**

court found the complainant's evidence to support their 'well-known' trademark insufficient, and ruled in favor for the respondent. However, the CDNDRC, Beijing's People's High Court, and Supreme People's Court, determined that the evidence showed that the respondent should have known

1. "Rushes to Statehood, The Oklahoma Land Runs". Dickinson Research Center. Retrieved 2014-05-09. 2. Reeves, Keir; Frost, Lionel; Fahey, Charles (2010). "Integrating the Historiography of the Nineteenth-Century Gold Rushes". *Australian Economic History Review* 50 (2): 111. 3. (ICANN, 2000). 4. & 5. Article 15 & 16 of CNDRP and rules
6. Article PRC'S Civil Procedure 7. New Rules for Resolving Chinese Domain Name Disputes - A Comparative Analysis Richard WuSchool of LawUniversity of Hong Kong 8. New Rules for Resolving Chinese Domain Name Disputes - A Comparative Analysis Richard WuSchool of LawUniversity of Hong Kong 9. Rule 2(2) CDNDRP and rules 10. CDNDRP and rules 11. "Contracting Parties to the Paris Convention". WIPO. Retrieved 2012-12-30.

12. http://www.wipo.int/treaties/en/text.jsp?file_id=288514 Paris Conventionfor the Protection of Industrial Property of March 20, 1883,as revised at Brussels on December 14, 1900,at Washington on June 2, 1911,at The Hague on November 6, 1925,at London on June 2, 1934,at Lisbon on October 31, 1958,and at Stockholm on July 14, 1967,and as amended on September 28, 1979 13. See id. 14. Alternative Dispute Resolution, An Essential Competency for Lawyers, by Mark V.B. Partridge **Oxford University Press (2009).** 15. http://www.ccpit-patent.com.cn/references/Law_Against_Unfair_Competition_China.htm law Against Unfair Competition of The People's Republic of China (Adopted at the Third Session of the Standing Committee of the Eighth National People's Congress on September 2, 1993. Promulgated by Order No. 10 of the President of the People's Republic of China on September 2, 1993. and Effective as of December 1, General Principles of THE Civil Law of the People's Republic of China (Adopted on April 12, 1986) **16, 17, & 18.** Alternative Dispute Resolution, An Essential Competency for Lawyers, by Mark V.B. Partridge **Oxford University Press (2009).**

that the trademark was 'well-known' according to Subparagraph (c) of Article 5 of The Anti-Unfair Competition Law in China. And in <u>Procter & Gamble Company v. Shnhai Chenxuan Technology and Trade Co. Ltd</u>, the complainant provided evidence of the trademark

1. "Rushes to Statehood, The Oklahoma Land Runs". Dickinson Research Center. Retrieved 2014-05-09. **2.** Reeves, Keir; Frost, Lionel; Fahey, Charles (2010). "Integrating the Historiography of the Nineteenth-Century Gold Rushes". *Australian Economic History Review* **50** (2): 111. **3.** (ICANN, 2000). **4. & 5.** Article 15 & 16 of CNDRP and rules
6. Article PRC'S Civil Procedure **7.** New Rules for Resolving Chinese Domain Name Disputes - A Comparative Analysis Richard WuSchool of LawUniversity of Hong Kong **8**. New Rules for Resolving Chinese Domain Name Disputes - A Comparative Analysis Richard WuSchool of LawUniversity of Hong Kong **9.** Rule 2(2) CDNDRP and rules **10.** CDNDRP and rules **11.** "Contracting Parties to the Paris Convention". WIPO. Retrieved 2012-12-30.

12. http://www.wipo.int/treaties/en/text.jsp?file_id=288514 Paris Conventionfor the Protection of Industrial Property of March 20, 1883,as revised at Brussels on December 14, 1900,at Washington on June 2, 1911,at The Hague on November 6, 1925,at London on June 2, 1934,at Lisbon on October 31, 1958,and at Stockholm on July 14, 1967,and as amended on September 28, 1979 **13.** See id. **14.** Alternative Dispute Resolution, An Essential Competency for Lawyers, by Mark V.B. Partridge **Oxford University Press (2009). 15.** http://www.ccpit-patent.com.cn/references/Law_Against_Unfair_Competition_China.htm law Against Unfair Competition of The People's Republic of China (Adopted at the Third Session of the Standing Committee of the Eighth National People's Congress on September 2, 1993. Promulgated by Order No. 10 of the President of the People's Republic of China on September 2, 1993. and Effective as of December 1, General Principles of THE Civil Law of the People's Republic of China (Adopted on April 12, 1986) **16, 17, & 18.** Alternative Dispute Resolution, An Essential Competency for Lawyers, by Mark V.B. Partridge **Oxford University Press (2009).**

being used for many years on packaging, provided the costs of advertisements, awards by the Department of Domestic Trade for the product containing the trademark, awards by magazines for the product containing the trademark, and statistics and research showing the product

1. "Rushes to Statehood, The Oklahoma Land Runs". Dickinson Research Center. Retrieved 2014-05-09. 2. Reeves, Keir; Frost, Lionel; Fahey, Charles (2010). "Integrating the Historiography of the Nineteenth-Century Gold Rushes". *Australian Economic History Review* 50 (2): 111. 3. (ICANN, 2000). 4. & 5. Article 15 & 16 of CNDRP and rules
6. Article PRC'S Civil Procedure 7. New Rules for Resolving Chinese Domain Name Disputes - A Comparative Analysis Richard WuSchool of LawUniversity of Hong Kong 8. New Rules for Resolving Chinese Domain Name Disputes - A Comparative Analysis Richard WuSchool of LawUniversity of Hong Kong 9. Rule 2(2) CDNDRP and rules 10. CDNDRP and rules 11. "Contracting Parties to the Paris Convention". WIPO. Retrieved 2012-12-30.

12. http://www.wipo.int/treaties/en/text.jsp?file_id=288514 Paris Conventionfor the Protection of Industrial Property of March 20, 1883,as revised at Brussels on December 14, 1900,at Washington on June 2, 1911,at The Hague on November 6, 1925,at London on June 2, 1934,at Lisbon on October 31, 1958,and at Stockholm on July 14, 1967,and as amended on September 28, 1979 13. See id. 14. Alternative Dispute Resolution, An Essential Competency for Lawyers, by Mark V.B. Partridge **Oxford University Press (2009).** 15. http://www.ccpit-patent.com.cn/references/Law_Against_Unfair_Competition_China.htm law Against Unfair Competition of The People's Republic of China (Adopted at the Third Session of the Standing Committee of the Eighth National People's Congress on September 2, 1993. Promulgated by Order No. 10 of the President of the People's Republic of China on September 2, 1993. and Effective as of December 1, General Principles of THE Civil Law of the People's Republic of China (Adopted on April 12, 1986) **16, 17, & 18.** Alternative Dispute Resolution, An Essential Competency for Lawyers, by Mark V.B. Partridge **Oxford University Press (2009).**

highly ranked by experts by companies located in China. The CDNDRC and court found in favor of the complainant stating that they should have known the trademark was well known, regardless that they were not apart of the same industry practice.

1. "Rushes to Statehood, The Oklahoma Land Runs". Dickinson Research Center. Retrieved 2014-05-09. 2. Reeves, Keir; Frost, Lionel; Fahey, Charles (2010). "Integrating the Historiography of the Nineteenth-Century Gold Rushes". *Australian Economic History Review* 50 (2): 111. 3. (ICANN, 2000). 4. & 5. Article 15 & 16 of CNDRP and rules
6. Article PRC'S Civil Procedure 7. New Rules for Resolving Chinese Domain Name Disputes - A Comparative Analysis Richard WuSchool of LawUniversity of Hong Kong 8. New Rules for Resolving Chinese Domain Name Disputes - A Comparative Analysis Richard WuSchool of LawUniversity of Hong Kong 9. Rule 2(2) CDNDRP and rules 10. CDNDRP and rules 11. "Contracting Parties to the Paris Convention". WIPO. Retrieved 2012-12-30.

12. http://www.wipo.int/treaties/en/text.jsp?file_id=288514 Paris Conventionfor the Protection of Industrial Property of March 20, 1883,as revised at Brussels on December 14, 1900,at Washington on June 2, 1911,at The Hague on November 6, 1925,at London on June 2, 1934,at Lisbon on October 31, 1958,and at Stockholm on July 14, 1967,and as amended on September 28, 1979 13. See id. 14. Alternative Dispute Resolution, An Essential Competency for Lawyers, by Mark V.B. Partridge Oxford University Press (2009). 15. http://www.ccpit-patent.com.cn/references/Law_Against_Unfair_Competition_China.htm law Against Unfair Competition of The People's Republic of China (Adopted at the Third Session of the Standing Committee of the Eighth National People's Congress on September 2, 1993. Promulgated by Order No. 10 of the President of the People's Republic of China on September 2, 1993. and Effective as of December 1, General Principles of THE Civil Law of the People's Republic of China (Adopted on April 12, 1986) 16, 17, & 18. Alternative Dispute Resolution, An Essential Competency for Lawyers, by Mark V.B. Partridge Oxford University Press (2009).

However in <u>Madonna Ciccone, v. Dan Parisi</u>, the respondent sited a pervious case, <u>Sting v. Michael Urvan</u>, claiming he had made a bona fide use of the name before obtaining the domain name registration, and there was no indication that he was seeking to trade on the goodwill of the

1. "Rushes to Statehood, The Oklahoma Land Runs". Dickinson Research Center. Retrieved 2014-05-09. 2. Reeves, Keir; Frost, Lionel; Fahey, Charles (2010). "Integrating the Historiography of the Nineteenth-Century Gold Rushes". *Australian Economic History Review* **50** (2): 111. 3. (ICANN, 2000). 4. & 5. Article 15 & 16 of CNDRP and rules
6. Article PRC'S Civil Procedure 7. New Rules for Resolving Chinese Domain Name Disputes - A Comparative Analysis Richard WuSchool of LawUniversity of Hong Kong 8. New Rules for Resolving Chinese Domain Name Disputes - A Comparative Analysis Richard WuSchool of LawUniversity of Hong Kong 9. Rule 2(2) CDNDRP and rules 10. CDNDRP and rules 11. "Contracting Parties to the Paris Convention". WIPO. Retrieved 2012-12-30.

12. http://www.wipo.int/treaties/en/text.jsp?file_id=288514 Paris Conventionfor the Protection of Industrial Property of March 20, 1883,as revised at Brussels on December 14, 1900,at Washington on June 2, 1911,at The Hague on November 6, 1925,at London on June 2, 1934,at Lisbon on October 31, 1958,and at Stockholm on July 14, 1967,and as amended on September 28, 1979 13. See id. 14. Alternative Dispute Resolution, An Essential Competency for Lawyers, by Mark V.B. Partridge **Oxford University Press (2009).** 15. http://www.ccpit-patent.com.cn/references/Law_Against_Unfair_Competition_China.htm law Against Unfair Competition of The People's Republic of China (Adopted at the Third Session of the Standing Committee of the Eighth National People's Congress on September 2, 1993. Promulgated by Order No. 10 of the President of the People's Republic of China on September 2, 1993. and Effective as of December 1, General Principles of THE Civil Law of the People's Republic of China (Adopted on April 12, 1986) **16, 17, & 18.** Alternative Dispute Resolution, An Essential Competency for Lawyers, by Mark V.B. Partridge **Oxford University Press (2009).**

'well-known' singer" (17). The court held that the respondent has offered no alternative explanation for adopting the name for the website: no explaining why madonna.com was worth $20,000, why it was valuable as an attraction for a sexually explicit web site, or made no tie in his web site to

1. "Rushes to Statehood, The Oklahoma Land Runs". Dickinson Research Center. Retrieved 2014-05-09. 2. Reeves, Keir; Frost, Lionel; Fahey, Charles (2010). "Integrating the Historiography of the Nineteenth-Century Gold Rushes". *Australian Economic History Review* 50 (2): 111. 3. (ICANN, 2000). 4. & 5. Article 15 & 16 of CNDRP and rules

6. Article PRC'S Civil Procedure 7. New Rules for Resolving Chinese Domain Name Disputes - A Comparative Analysis Richard WuSchool of LawUniversity of Hong Kong 8. New Rules for Resolving Chinese Domain Name Disputes - A Comparative Analysis Richard WuSchool of LawUniversity of Hong Kong 9. Rule 2(2) CDNDRP and rules 10. CDNDRP and rules 11. "Contracting Parties to the Paris Convention". WIPO. Retrieved 2012-12-30.

12. http://www.wipo.int/treaties/en/text.jsp?file_id=288514 Paris Conventionfor the Protection of Industrial Property of March 20, 1883,as revised at Brussels on December 14, 1900,at Washington on June 2, 1911,at The Hague on November 6, 1925,at London on June 2, 1934,at Lisbon on October 31, 1958,and at Stockholm on July 14, 1967,and as amended on September 28, 1979 13. See id. 14. Alternative Dispute Resolution, An Essential Competency for Lawyers, by Mark V.B. Partridge **Oxford University Press (2009).** 15. http://www.ccpit-patent.com.cn/references/Law_Against_Unfair_Competition_China.htm law Against Unfair Competition of The People's Republic of China (Adopted at the Third Session of the Standing Committee of the Eighth National People's Congress on September 2, 1993. Promulgated by Order No. 10 of the President of the People's Republic of China on September 2, 1993. and Effective as of December 1, General Principles of THE Civil Law of the People's Republic of China (Adopted on April 12, 1986) 16, 17, & 18. Alternative Dispute Resolution, An Essential Competency for Lawyers, by Mark V.B. Partridge **Oxford University Press (2009).**

any dictionary definition of Madonna, therefore, the only plausible explanation was to trade upon the fame of the complainant's name and mark for commercial gain in bad faith.

4.   Damages

1. "Rushes to Statehood, The Oklahoma Land Runs". Dickinson Research Center. Retrieved 2014-05-09. 2. Reeves, Keir; Frost, Lionel; Fahey, Charles (2010). "Integrating the Historiography of the Nineteenth-Century Gold Rushes". *Australian Economic History Review* 50 (2): 111. 3. (ICANN, 2000). 4. & 5. Article 15 & 16 of CNDRP and rules

6. Article PRC'S Civil Procedure 7. New Rules for Resolving Chinese Domain Name Disputes - A Comparative Analysis Richard WuSchool of LawUniversity of Hong Kong 8. New Rules for Resolving Chinese Domain Name Disputes - A Comparative Analysis Richard WuSchool of LawUniversity of Hong Kong 9. Rule 2(2) CDNDRP and rules 10. CDNDRP and rules 11. "Contracting Parties to the Paris Convention". WIPO. Retrieved 2012-12-30.

12. http://www.wipo.int/treaties/en/text.jsp?file_id=288514 Paris Conventionfor the Protection of Industrial Property of March 20, 1883,as revised at Brussels on December 14, 1900,at Washington on June 2, 1911,at The Hague on November 6, 1925,at London on June 2, 1934,at Lisbon on October 31, 1958,and at Stockholm on July 14, 1967,and as amended on September 28, 1979 13. See id. 14. Alternative Dispute Resolution, An Essential Competency for Lawyers, by Mark V.B. Partridge **Oxford University Press (2009). 15.** http://www.ccpit-patent.com.cn/references/Law_Against_Unfair_Competition_China.htm law Against Unfair Competition of The People's Republic of China (Adopted at the Third Session of the Standing Committee of the Eighth National People's Congress on September 2, 1993. Promulgated by Order No. 10 of the President of the People's Republic of China on September 2, 1993. and Effective as of December 1, General Principles of THE Civil Law of the People's Republic of China (Adopted on April 12, 1986) **16, 17, & 18.** Alternative Dispute Resolution, An Essential Competency for Lawyers, by Mark V.B. Partridge **Oxford University Press (2009).**

Has the domain name holder caused any damages by infringing on the trademark owner's IPR's. However, if the trademark owner can prove that the trademark is 'well-known' this factor will not apply (18).

III. Conclusion

1. "Rushes to Statehood, The Oklahoma Land Runs". Dickinson Research Center. Retrieved 2014-05-09. 2. Reeves, Keir; Frost, Lionel; Fahey, Charles (2010). "Integrating the Historiography of the Nineteenth-Century Gold Rushes". *Australian Economic History Review* 50 (2): 111. 3. (ICANN, 2000). 4. & 5. Article 15 & 16 of CNDRP and rules
6. Article PRC'S Civil Procedure 7. New Rules for Resolving Chinese Domain Name Disputes - A Comparative Analysis Richard WuSchool of LawUniversity of Hong Kong 8. New Rules for Resolving Chinese Domain Name Disputes - A Comparative Analysis Richard WuSchool of LawUniversity of Hong Kong 9. Rule 2(2) CDNDRP and rules 10. CDNDRP and rules 11. "Contracting Parties to the Paris Convention". WIPO. Retrieved 2012-12-30.

12. http://www.wipo.int/treaties/en/text.jsp?file_id=288514 Paris Conventionfor the Protection of Industrial Property of March 20, 1883,as revised at Brussels on December 14, 1900,at Washington on June 2, 1911,at The Hague on November 6, 1925,at London on June 2, 1934,at Lisbon on October 31, 1958,and at Stockholm on July 14, 1967,and as amended on September 28, 1979 13. See id. 14. Alternative Dispute Resolution, An Essential Competency for Lawyers, by Mark V.B. Partridge **Oxford University Press (2009).** 15. http://www.ccpit-patent.com.cn/references/Law_Against_Unfair_Competition_China.htm law Against Unfair Competition of The People's Republic of China (Adopted at the Third Session of the Standing Committee of the Eighth National People's Congress on September 2, 1993. Promulgated by Order No. 10 of the President of the People's Republic of China on September 2, 1993. and Effective as of December 1, General Principles of THE Civil Law of the People's Republic of China (Adopted on April 12, 1986) **16, 17, & 18.** Alternative Dispute Resolution, An Essential Competency for Lawyers, by Mark V.B. Partridge **Oxford University Press (2009).**

Oklahoma's Land Rush of 1889 and 1893 and the Gold Rushes told a particular tale, what does the Great Domain Rush tell us about China? Perhaps, it tells us something about our global economy. Each domain is a stake to a claim, and globalism continues its reach through the Internet to

1. "Rushes to Statehood, The Oklahoma Land Runs". Dickinson Research Center. Retrieved 2014-05-09. 2. Reeves, Keir; Frost, Lionel; Fahey, Charles (2010). "Integrating the Historiography of the Nineteenth-Century Gold Rushes". *Australian Economic History Review* 50 (2): 111. 3. (ICANN, 2000). 4. & 5. Article 15 & 16 of CNDRP and rules
6. Article PRC'S Civil Procedure 7. New Rules for Resolving Chinese Domain Name Disputes - A Comparative Analysis Richard WuSchool of LawUniversity of Hong Kong 8. New Rules for Resolving Chinese Domain Name Disputes - A Comparative Analysis Richard WuSchool of LawUniversity of Hong Kong 9. Rule 2(2) CDNDRP and rules 10. CDNDRP and rules 11. "Contracting Parties to the Paris Convention". WIPO. Retrieved 2012-12-30.

12. http://www.wipo.int/treaties/en/text.jsp?file_id=288514 Paris Conventionfor the Protection of Industrial Property of March 20, 1883,as revised at Brussels on December 14, 1900,at Washington on June 2, 1911,at The Hague on November 6, 1925,at London on June 2, 1934,at Lisbon on October 31, 1958,and at Stockholm on July 14, 1967,and as amended on September 28, 1979 13. See id. 14. Alternative Dispute Resolution, An Essential Competency for Lawyers, by Mark V.B. Partridge **Oxford University Press (2009).** 15. http://www.ccpit-patent.com.cn/references/Law_Against_Unfair_Competition_China.htm law Against Unfair Competition of The People's Republic of China (Adopted at the Third Session of the Standing Committee of the Eighth National People's Congress on September 2, 1993. Promulgated by Order No. 10 of the President of the People's Republic of China on September 2, 1993. and Effective as of December 1, General Principles of THE Civil Law of the People's Republic of China (Adopted on April 12, 1986) **16, 17, & 18.** Alternative Dispute Resolution, An Essential Competency for Lawyers, by Mark V.B. Partridge **Oxford University Press (2009).**

China. If you are going to stake a claim to a particular domain name, you had better back it up with a valid commercial enterprise or personality, and make sure it is unique. Like the land in Oklahoma and various other parts containing Gold deposits, the land had to be put to use, and as is painfully

1. "Rushes to Statehood, The Oklahoma Land Runs". Dickinson Research Center. Retrieved 2014-05-09. 2. Reeves, Keir; Frost, Lionel; Fahey, Charles (2010). "Integrating the Historiography of the Nineteenth-Century Gold Rushes". *Australian Economic History Review* 50 (2): 111. 3. (ICANN, 2000). 4. & 5. Article 15 & 16 of CNDRP and rules
6. Article PRC'S Civil Procedure 7. New Rules for Resolving Chinese Domain Name Disputes - A Comparative Analysis Richard WuSchool of LawUniversity of Hong Kong 8. New Rules for Resolving Chinese Domain Name Disputes - A Comparative Analysis Richard WuSchool of LawUniversity of Hong Kong 9. Rule 2(2) CDNDRP and rules 10. CDNDRP and rules 11. "Contracting Parties to the Paris Convention". WIPO. Retrieved 2012-12-30.

12. http://www.wipo.int/treaties/en/text.jsp?file_id=288514 Paris Conventionfor the Protection of Industrial Property of March 20, 1883,as revised at Brussels on December 14, 1900,at Washington on June 2, 1911,at The Hague on November 6, 1925,at London on June 2, 1934,at Lisbon on October 31, 1958,and at Stockholm on July 14, 1967,and as amended on September 28, 1979 13. See id. 14. Alternative Dispute Resolution, An Essential Competency for Lawyers, by Mark V.B. Partridge Oxford University Press (2009). 15. http://www.ccpit-patent.com.cn/references/Law_Against_Unfair_Competition_China.htm law Against Unfair Competition of The People's Republic of China (Adopted at the Third Session of the Standing Committee of the Eighth National People's Congress on September 2, 1993. Promulgated by Order No. 10 of the President of the People's Republic of China on September 2, 1993. and Effective as of December 1, General Principles of THE Civil Law of the People's Republic of China (Adopted on April 12, 1986) 16, 17, & 18. Alternative Dispute Resolution, An Essential Competency for Lawyers, by Mark V.B. Partridge Oxford University Press (2009).

obvious even in the cyber world, there are no squatting rights.

1. "Rushes to Statehood, The Oklahoma Land Runs". Dickinson Research Center. Retrieved 2014-05-09. **2.** Reeves, Keir; Frost, Lionel; Fahey, Charles (2010). "Integrating the Historiography of the Nineteenth-Century Gold Rushes". *Australian Economic History Review* **50** (2): 111. **3.** (ICANN, 2000). **4. & 5.** Article 15 & 16 of CNDRP and rules
6. Article PRC'S Civil Procedure **7.** New Rules for Resolving Chinese Domain Name Disputes - A Comparative Analysis Richard WuSchool of LawUniversity of Hong Kong **8.** New Rules for Resolving Chinese Domain Name Disputes - A Comparative Analysis Richard WuSchool of LawUniversity of Hong Kong **9.** Rule 2(2) CDNDRP and rules **10.** CDNDRP and rules **11.** "Contracting Parties to the Paris Convention". WIPO. Retrieved 2012-12-30.

12. http://www.wipo.int/treaties/en/text.jsp?file_id=288514 Paris Conventionfor the Protection of Industrial Property of March 20, 1883,as revised at Brussels on December 14, 1900,at Washington on June 2, 1911,at The Hague on November 6, 1925,at London on June 2, 1934,at Lisbon on October 31, 1958,and at Stockholm on July 14, 1967,and as amended on September 28, 1979 **13.** See id. **14.** Alternative Dispute Resolution, An Essential Competency for Lawyers, by Mark V.B. Partridge **Oxford University Press (2009). 15.** http://www.ccpit-patent.com.cn/references/Law_Against_Unfair_Competition_China.htm law Against Unfair Competition of The People's Republic of China (Adopted at the Third Session of the Standing Committee of the Eighth National People's Congress on September 2, 1993. Promulgated by Order No. 10 of the President of the People's Republic of China on September 2, 1993. and Effective as of December 1, General Principles of THE Civil Law of the People's Republic of China (Adopted on April 12, 1986) **16, 17, & 18.** Alternative Dispute Resolution, An Essential Competency for Lawyers, by Mark V.B. Partridge **Oxford University Press (2009).**

www.ingramcontent.com/pod-product-compliance
Lightning Source LLC
Chambersburg PA
CBHW030019190526
45157CB00016B/3133